WHAT if ? YOU CAN!

ESCAPE from WAS

by toniraye

the Peppertree Press
Sarasota, Florida

Published by *the* Peppertree Press, LLC.

Cover design by Crush Branding and Design, LLC
Graphic design by Susan Kirk
Editing by Jodie Brown and Bonita Fieser

For information regarding permission,
call 941-922-2662 or contact us at our website:
www.peppertreepublishing.com or write to:
the Peppertree Press, LLC.
Attention: Publisher
1269 First Street, Suite 7
Sarasota, Florida 34236

ISBN: 978-1-936051-30-4
Library of Congress Number: 2009938054

Printed in the United States of America
Printed October 2009

Dedication

This book is written in loving memory of Bill Riedler.
Bill's dedication and determination to make the world a better place
caused me to realize my own potential,
and that my life and every life matters.

To this special mentor and teacher
who isn't with us anymore
I simply wish to say:
Thank you for teaching me that
the gift I am—is the gift I Am!

Most especially to my
precious son
and grandchildren
who daily teach me the
true meaning of Legacy.

ESCAPE FROM WAS

Contents

Introduction

My agent told me to write an introduction for the book you hold in your hands. I think I'm supposed to write about how great the book is and entice you to trade your hard earned dollars at the cash register for my best seller. I want to be enticing (I really do), but no matter what I tell of the scope of this story, that will not be the whole of the story. To get the meaning beneath the meaning you must first look inward.

Who are you? Who are you for the people in your life? How has your environment, the world culture, your ethnic culture, and the kinds of jobs your parents had shaped your view of yourself and the world around you?

I was born, you were born, into a conversation.
This conversation is both shouts and whispers.
It is unwritten rules that shape us,
mold us into who we are and what is possible for us to be.

The already existing conversation tells us
what is, and isn't, possible in our world.
This conversation is often about how to fit into
an already existing framework of mediocrity.

The day of our birth, we were each a bright promise of the future. Little by little as we learned that 2 + 2 = 4, we misplaced the magic we were born to be. It didn't disappear all at once and it didn't disappear forever. It is lost in the daily grind we call life.

This book offers practical ways we can *marry our intentions to equal the results we say we want.* This book is about how to change limiting belief conversations in our world, our culture, and our own life.

Are you ready to create your future? To be free from the despotic rule of your circumstances? This book is about the connection between Pure Joy and Free Will. As you yoke your intentions with clarity and action, you are powerful beyond measure. In fact, you have the power to create a legacy for future generations, inspiring them to create their own new and greater possibilities. Each generation has the ability to launch future generations forward.

It is not a question of whether we will leave a legacy. It is a matter of what legacy we will leave. The question for each of us is this: what legacy do I intend to leave and what way of *being* will make that happen? What legacy will you create for your children and their children to come?

How to create from nothing. The word *create* means to bring forth from nothing. From what doesn't exist and isn't possible to exist, we can create something into existence.

Who we are "being" creates what we will do.
What we do creates what we have.
You are a Being-Doing-Having machine.
With conscious intention and commitment,
you can Be-Do-Have on purpose.

You are about to explore how one girl, one woman, one boy, one man began a journey to create and live in the Land of Becoming. If night after night, you put your head on the pillow, weighed down with the cares of life, then you are living in the Land of Was. It's time to wake up and realize that today is different from yesterday. Today, we have the power to change. The opportunity to create. To realize that:

I am created from nothing.
I am no thing.
I am no fixed thing.

If I am not the way I was,
then I am on my way to becoming
the me I interpret and invent myself
to be moment to moment.
The context of who I am
is simply who I say I am.

To create my future,
to bring my intentions and desires into existence,
to create and change the future of the world
I don't need anyone's permission.
I don't need anyone's agreement.
I only need to be aware that I live in an
ever occurring, changing,
evolving world.
By gosh and by golly,
guess what?

I am, you are, the creator of the game of your life!
I can't create this future,
this important game called *My Life,*
out of what I already know,
because what I know already *Is,*
and what already *Is,*
Is already created.

What's the bottom line?
I don't want to create what Is.
What already Is—is fixed in place.
Therefore, what *Is—Is already a Was,*

and what *Was* won't bring us new results.
We can't create what Was
for that Is already created.

What Was has created the results you have right now.
Why would you want to set an intention
for the results you already have?

I'm not suggesting that the results you have right now are bad.
But you've already got 'em so why create
the same 'ole thing over and over again?
Why not set a new intention
for what you are committed to in this new moment?

Hey there!
You!
Yeah, *YOU*
can create a brand new something
just because you decide to.
Just because you can!

Even as you read this sentence
you are already creating a new, fluid,
constantly changing,
wondrously evolving,
moment to moment
Occurring you.
You will never be the Was you were five minutes ago,
because in this instant the idea already *Occurs* to you
that you can be, and have, something new.

In the conceptual moment that it *Occurs* to you
to live in an *Occurring* world,
you are reinvented and changed forever.

If you put down this book,
if you don't understand the jargon of these words,
it matters not
because the idea of seeing yourself as an
Occurring being
has already changed the way it Was.

We are always on our way to becoming a bright, new, occurring possibility. You and I are always and forever on our way to becoming a newly created human being.
This book is about the marriage between
Our intention *(Context)*
and
our results *(Content).*

Have a wonderful time reading and realizing the possibility that you are.
The moment you see that you were born
to the marriage between
Pure Joy with Free Will
you will understand the possibility
and magnitude of power at your disposal.

Once we realize that we are simply and profoundly
interpretation all the way to the core
of who we are,
then as individuals and as a species
we will be ready to be
100 percent responsible,
100 percent of the time
for the results in our life.
You will attract any results you desire!

Hugs and best of possibilities to you,
toniraye

~ toniraye.com ~

Before The Beginning

Not long ago, I was broke, divorced, and owed $90 thousand to the Internal Revenue Service. I was firmly rooted and living poorly in the Land of Was. My situation appeared hopeless. Today my life is flourishing and I'm among the nation's top five percent of wage earners. I have the freedom to go where I want and do what I want, when I want. My address is in the Land of Becoming.

How did I relocate? How did I create a new lifestyle drastically better than the circumstances I found myself in a short time ago? The answer is in these pages. I invite you to observe the journey and, if you choose, follow me. **The path is repeatable. You can make the move. Beginning today.**

Part I presents a story of growing up in the Land of Was. The story incidents will trigger memories of events that happened to you. The end result is that we all end up in the Land of Was.

This modern day fable deals with philosophical beliefs. At times you may need to suspend your belief about what a child would say or think. The tale is about a young girl and a young boy. Remember, there is a young girl and a young boy inside each of us. The story represents our inner child and how we formed our adult core and, usually hidden, belief systems.

On the surface the story is simple. You may think of your own history as dramatic and complicated. However, when I look below the surface of my own life, when I strip away my mistaken interpretation of events, I find that life is relatively simple. Each of us repeat a few dramas with many variations.

The simple analogy allows us to peek below the surface and imagine a whole new way to reinvent our lives and all of our limiting belief conversations.

Part II presents principles and insights for living in the Land of Becoming. I suggest you read through this section and then come back to implement parts that are pertinent for your personal growth.

Once again there is no right way. The best course of action will occur to you as you begin the process.

Part III presents specific exercises and a private journal. This area encourages and supports you to uncover hidden belief systems that hold you back from having your fully realized, most powerful intentions show up in life.

PART I

A MODERN DAY FABLE ABOUT LIVING IN THE LAND OF WAS

Beware—
You are about to enter the Land of Was

If it is today and it was yesterday,
then you can take it to the bank.
That's the way it Was and ever shall be.
There is no possibility
because you are a fixed,
set-in-place, programmed system of beliefs.
That's just the way it is
living in the Land of Was.

As In Any Land There Are Rules

If you don't know the rules, you can't win the game.
The Rules Aren't Written Down Anywhere
But Don't Kid Yourself—
We All Know THERE ARE RULES!

The rules only work when the following foundational beliefs remain intact:

1. The name of the game is survival.
2. Life is a test.
3. I don't matter and I am disposable because someday I will die and then I will be replaced and forgotten forever.
4. In order to survive, I must always (and I mean ALWAYS)
   a) Look good
   b) Be right
   c) Be in control
5. I am afraid because someone is out to get me. It's normal to be afraid but for gosh sakes cover it up.
6. Everybody has their own agenda and no one but me actually has my best interests at heart.

THE RULES FOR SURVIVAL LIVING IN THE LAND OF WAS

1) In order for me to win, someone has to lose.

2) Have-Do-Be. I must HAVE stuff, and work hard, in order to BE what I want to BE. If I work hard and do the right thing, then someday it will be my turn.
   (a) As soon as I have the right __________ (house, car, wife, husband, kids, etc.)
   (b) Then I'll do the things that cool people with beautiful houses and cars do.
   (c) Then I'll be ______________ (happy, powerful, joyous, committed, etc.)

3) I must climb the vertical ladder. There is always another rung to climb on the vertical ladder.

4) There is no place to rest or renew on the vertical climb because someone is always waiting to climb into my spot.

5) I am always ahead of (above) some people on the ladder. I'm definitely better than "those people".

6) There are always people above me on the ladder but they are "jerks."

7) More-Better-Different
   (a) I need to have more and do more.
   (b) Then and only then I will be better than others.
   (c) Once I am better than "those people" things will be different.
   (d) Once things are different, then I'll be happy.

8) I compare myself to my past.

9) I compare myself to my expectations and what I think I should be.

10) I compare myself to others.

11) Stress is a daily part of life.

12) I make promises to myself and others based on my feelings and circumstances.

13) It's acceptable to break a promise as long as I have a good excuse.

14) My stock phrase is, "Yeah, but ..."

15) My focus is on me, my history, my circumstances.

16) I constantly wonder:
What's wrong with me?

What's wrong with them?
What's wrong with it?

17) I believe that things and people are locked into certain roles.
Judgments and assessments follow, such as:
Men are ______________________.
Women are ____________________.
The world is ___________________.
Therefore, I must be______________.

18) I make no distinction between the facts and my story about what happened.

19) Career and relationships are something to do, things to get through.

20) A frequent phrase about my life is, "I have to…."

Escape From Was

Once upon a time in the Land of Was, two children were born on the same day, at nearly the same moment. One was a boy, the other a girl. Both were lucky, born not only healthy and whole, but to good parents of respectable families well known in the Land of Was. Their births brought great hope and promise: these two children would grow to be positive, productive citizens in the Land of Was.

A Naming Ceremony

As was the custom in The Land of Was, each set of parents immediately began the important task of naming their newborn child.

The girl was born to parents who proclaimed her to be precious and beautiful. She came packaged pretty as a picture with thick curly hair, bright eyes, and a smattering of freckles across her cute little nose. From the first day of her birth she had an impish smile and she was smart as can be. Oh, that little girl sure did like attention. She was talking up a storm by the age of 18 months, and once she started talking, she just never stopped.

How do I know these rumors are true?
Well, everyone in the Land of Was said so,
and with such reliable witnesses that certainly makes it true.
That is who she Was.

If everybody says so
and if it is today
and if it was yesterday,
then that's that—
that's the way it is in Was.

Anyway who cares if she wanted
a little too much attention?
So what if she talked too much?
In Was, it is considered quite precocious for girls to
be gregarious. That's just the way it is where girls are
concerned in Was.
Most all girls talk too much—isn't that so?
Just tune 'em out.
That's how we handle that in the Land of Was.

The girl's father was a carpenter, famous in Was for building grand traditional structures. Her mother was known as a forward-thinker (and thus someone to be respected, though not completely trusted), and it was the idea of the mother to name their child something special, something different.

At first, the husband was adamantly opposed to
anything except a normal, good, girl name.
But the mother lobbied long and hard,
and no one was really surprised
that after much discussion and debate
that the couple threw caution to the wind
and blessed their baby
with a very special name.

And that's how it happened:
on a bright sunny morning
her father gently lifted the girl into his arms
as they thanked the Truth within the Universe
for the whole and complete and perfect gift
they had been given.

And he most reverently proclaimed her name to be

Pure Joy.

Concerning the naming of the newborn boy, there was no discussion, no need for debate. There was no way on no day that they were going to give their strong healthy boy some off-the-wall special sort of name.

By gosh and by golly, what would people think?
In the Land of Was, names are important.
Why?
Are you crazy?
Don't ask why!

That's just the way it has always been in the Land of Was,
and who was anyone to argue?

Names are how children are framed and labeled
in the Land of Was.

In the Land of Was, names help people immediately know about a person. Categorizing and segmenting others keeps things calm and familiar. For in the Land of Was, comparing yourself to others and being alike has a degree of comfort to it. And while people often talk about *wanting* change or dreaming big dreams, it's easier to settle for the same.

"Why strive for more," they say to one another and to themselves, *"when you can settle for the same?"*

The little boy's father was named William, as was his father's father, and his great-grandfather. With such a fine boy's name, his parents were assured that he would fit right in. He would have a *"strong Will"* to help him succeed, just like his dad. And if he worked hard, and did all the right things—just like his dad—then someday Will's turn would come.

And so it was in the Land of Was
that the boy's parents reverently
proclaimed their precious boy

William.

Here is an opportunity to write and/or reflect on ways this story might relate to your own life or if you prefer simply read through the questions quickly and continue with the story. All questions asked throughout the book are designed to encourage you to reflect.

Questions:

1. Can you remember a time when you had no guilt and felt no remorse?

2. What if you were whole and complete in this exact second?
   (a) How would you feel and what way of being would be at the core of who you are? (Example = powerful, valuable, adventurous, etc.)
   (b) What would you do?
   (c) What would you have?

Now it must be said that when news of the new children's names reached the people in the Land of Was, there was both happiness and confusion. All were happy to learn of William's name, for that was how people were named in the Land of Was. But when the people heard the little girl's name, they were puzzled. Soon their confusion turned into anger. Pure Joy? Was that a fit name to be given in the Land of Was?

No!
Who were these parents, to break the rules?
The nerve!
Do they think that their child is special?
Even knowing that the mother was a forward-thinker,
the citizens of the Land of Was
continued to be perplexed and upset.
In the Land of Was, every child was regarded as the same.
Most kids were normal kids from good, normal families.
Well, maybe not all kids.
You know, some kids in some parts of town
were not the same,
but let's not dwell on that now.
The point here is that having
a special name shouldn't be allowed.

Questions:

1. How many children in your family?

   Which number were you?

2. When you were a child, what are 3 adjectives your family would use to describe you? She/he was ____, ____, ______. (e.g. shy, bratty, smart, athletic, slow, sweet, stubborn, etc.)

Elevator Magic

As the parents of Pure Joy wanted to celebrate her fifth birthday, it came to pass that they took a break from the drift of life in Was. They loaded up the car and headed out to visit some family members who had moved to the Land of Becoming.

The very second the car pulled into the drive,
experiencing great anticipation
and bushels full of glee,
Pure Joy leaped
from the back seat
and landed right in her Grandma's welcoming arms.

Everyone was happy as Grandma announced,
"We are off to the races.
We'll stay in a quite fine hotel.
How's that for fun in the sun?
'Cause one thing we can be sure of;
good things happen often
right here—right now
in the Land of Becoming."

"Let's set an intention and declare it as true.
That the legacy for our family
abounds with love,
passion,
creativity,
contribution,
good health,
and a sprinkle of wealth."

And so it was that on a warm sunny day in the month of March, they happily set out for the Gator National Car Races.

Questions:

1. As a child, did you ever experience being loved unconditionally? If so, by whom?

   Can you recall a specific time? Describe in detail.

2. Can you think of a time that you have loved yourself unconditionally?

From the Unlocked Diary of Pure Joy

Anyone can read these pages for they contain the thoughts and feelings of me, Pure Joy. It brings me joy to share my thoughts with just about the entire world and anyone else including Santa Claus, the Tooth Fairy, and friendly aliens from other planets. I don't need to lock away my diary and my thoughts, go ahead, read on, I'm an open book, it's okay.

Day One: At Grandma's House in the Land of Becoming.

Dear Diary,

I hope I never forget this day with Grandma in this really exciting life in the Land of Becoming.

I asked her why they call it such a funny name.
She said, "Well, dear child of my heart,
The whole world is an ever-changing,
ever-evolving world.
We are never what we were yesterday
Because we are always on our way to becoming
whatever we declare ourselves to be.
Both you, and I (and the rest of the world),
are growing and changing, evolving and occurring.
We aren't a finished, fixed thing,
because moment to moment
we are on our way to becoming.
We are all beings in the making."

Dear Diary,

Sometimes I don't exactly understand the mysteries of the universe that Grandma tells me about. But one thing I know for sure, I love my Grandma and she loves me. She says that all I have to do is be Pure Joy and the rest will happen when I'm ready.

Day Two: My Thoughts About Being at the Races With Grandma in the Land of Becoming.

Dear Diary,

Yes, yes, yes, we are at the races. It is very exciting. We rode in an elevator with glass sides. I could see for a zillion miles over the city. The elevator was crammed with people all going to the races just like me.

Daddy showed me which elevator button to push.

And guess what happened next?

I waved my arms,

and moments later, the elevator doors opened.

I was proud.

Daddy was proud of me,

Mom was proud,

and best of all, Grandma was proud.

I turned around to look at the crowd in the elevator. You know, just to make sure everyone knew how important the moment was. I took a deep breath and then I revealed my secret to them all.

"Did you see that?" I said.
"The elevator doors opened and I made that happen.
It just might be that I'm magical."

Later we went to dinner and the chef wore a big hat. He cooked everything right there at our table. He turned the onions into a volcano complete with fire spitting toward the heavens. Next, he flipped a shrimp right into his hat. I laughed and laughed. Can you imagine anything more funny than that?

It was so much fun that I couldn't sit still. I jumped down from my seat and climbed into Grandma's lap. I whispered in her ear, "Grandma, I think he's magical just like me, just like you."

When I said that, Grandma seemed sort of shocked and she said, "Wow, I didn't know that I am magical, too."

I told her, "Of course, you're magical. How could I be magical if you didn't teach me?"

Hours later, Grandma was still smiling when she came to tuck me in bed and kiss me good-night.

It's great to be me.
To know life is an adventure and safe,
because it's my legacy,
it's my birthright as Pure Joy.
I am born to family who LIVES in the Land of Becoming.

DAY THREE: MY THOUGHTS ABOUT HAVING A TEA PARTY IN THE LAND OF BECOMING.

Dear Diary,

When I heard Dad say, "I owe, I owe, so back to the rat race we go," I knew our visit was over. Now we are in the car riding back to the Land of Was.

Before we left this morning, I had time with Grandma.
We had a special tea party and we shared secrets.
I told her how I might be afraid of going up escalators.
She told me that people of magic
have more ways to enjoy life
than just riding on the escalator,
so I don't need to worry.

And then she told me some secrets-of-the-universe like:

1) *Pure Joy does not need to compare herself to others,*
2) *Pure Joy does not need to compare herself to her past,*
3) *Pure Joy does not need to compare herself to what should be,*

She said, "Pure Joy, never ever 'should' on yourself."
Isn't that too funny?

She kissed the tip of my nose, let me smell the fragrance of a sunshine yellow rose from her garden as she told me to always remember this:

Someday when I get really old,
like forty-five or something,
I might get worried and forget about
the Land of Becoming.
But if ever I feel sad, it would suddenly occur to me
that the Land of Becoming is in my own back yard.
I carry a road map to the Becoming world
inside my very own heart.
Then
we rolled on the grass
playing with her soft, roly-poly puppy.
She giggled and breathlessly shouted
toward the heavens one more piece of advice:
"Pure Joy, here is the key that will always let you enter
the Land of Becoming.
Have a profound, blissful experience
once a week, at least!"

Even if I don't understand everything Grandma tells me, I hope I can remember the way she was being today. It would be a shame to never know how magical I am, or to experience onion volcanoes, or rolling in the fresh, sweet grass.

Questions

1. Write about a time when you:
   (a) compared yourself to your past,
   (b) compared yourself to what should be, and/or
   (c) compared yourself to someone else.

2. How do the comparisons cause you to feel about yourself? (e.g. not good enough or better than others, etc.)

3. Now, try to remember back to a time when you were innocent (not cynical) when you were willing to share of yourself and your ideas.

4. When was your last profound blissful experience? Describe in detail.

A Note from Pure Joy to You the Reader
Pure Joy Creates Destiny

Dear Reader,

You've seen baby pictures of yourself, yes? Mine are hilarious. There I am, this little round-faced girl in a frilly, pink lace dress. How lucky I was, to be born perfect, whole and healthy. No one taught me how to breathe, how to eat, how to digest. I could do everything naturally.

With my parents, I had everything.

I also had an ability which you possess as well. I could learn. The slightest object held me spellbound. A fuzzy caterpillar on a leaf. A piece of yellow corn. My amazing little hands. I learned to make sounds. At first, like you, I could only cry. (And I'm quite proud to say that I mastered crying quickly and, according to my parents, quite well.) Then I made other sounds. I laughed. I cooed. I grunted. I farted.

Babies do fart, you know. You fart, don't you? Of course, knowing about farting and talking about it are different. But pleaseeeeee, even if we are in Was, can't we get real sometimes? Saying what I thought and blurting out the truth came naturally before I knew about this rule:

"Don't tell people the truth.
Just tell them what they want to hear,
and for gosh sakes, always be polite."

Actually, I have never been clear on how the "always tell the truth" rule works with that other rule about just tell people what they want to hear, but one way or another you figure out about opposing rules if you want to avoid being a social outcast in Was. A fast learner, soon I could babble. And babble I did, babbling with the best of them. Even today, should you find yourself in the Land of Was, you will hear stories from friends and neighbors about my babbling.

While my babbling was legendary, that was nothing compared to my talking. As young as twelve months, according to my parents, I was talking up a storm.

Did I always understand what I was saying? Of course not. But that didn't stop me. I talked to my parents. I talked to my grandmama. I talked to my teddy bear and my spoon and the birds singing in the trees outside my bedroom window. I talked to everyone and everything, but most especially I loved to talk to my best friend, William, who lived across the street.

Will loves adventures and pirates and I think he will be a knight in shining armor when he becomes man-sized. But Will didn't much like to play tea party, and he would sometimes be off climbing the oak tree in his back yard. On those days when Will wasn't around, I'd talk to my other best friend who was very magical because she was completely invisible to everyone but me.

Her name was Destiny. I think Destiny is almost as good a name as Pure Joy. We chatted during tea parties of Kool-Aid and cookies. We told stories while building castles in my sand box. We whispered secrets to each other late at night snuggled under the covers in my bed when I should have been asleep. My Destiny listened to me completely and without judgment. I could share me and she never once laughed at any of my hopes, or dreams, or fears. She understood me quite perfectly, maybe even better than I understood myself.

The biggest dream I shared when I created my Destiny was how I was going to grow up and become a great artist. I got my creativity from my parents. My dad builds amazing stuff out of stone, steel, glass, and wood. When he finishes working on an old piece of mahogany, it truly is a thing of majestic beauty. I think I have my dad's creative genius.

Okay, okay, I know better now. In the Land of Was I can't create destiny because destiny doesn't exist. All the adults in my life say she's not real. I guess I should listen because others who have already been here and done that in Was know what's possible and what isn't.

The good news, at least I think it's good news, is that if I just work hard enough, if I just do the right thing, then someday it will be my turn.

Later, with a sad heart, I went to the attic, opened an old suitcase, put a doll inside that reminded me of my special friend Destiny, and shut the lid. It's a shame that we have to lock away our dreams and destiny in a dusty old trunk but if I want to grow up I guess that's just the way of it in The Land Of Was.

Certainly I won't repeat this to Mrs. Doom and Mrs. Gloom who live down the street, but in the quiet stillness of *the night I still remember the dreams I shared with my own Destiny. Every so often I think about not just drifting into an already Was existence but of creating my own Destiny out of my own Pure Joy self.*

Questions:

1. What are three dreams you had for your life when you were a child?

2. Write about a time in your life when you settled for less than what you wanted.
   (a) Did you argue and then give up?
   (b) Did you just never get started?
   (c) Did you feel angry, sad, nothing?
   (d) Pretend that you sabotaged yourself from getting the result you wanted. How did you do that? Why?

From the Computerized Journal of Will

Memo: From Will to Will

Regarding: To remind me about never getting sent to the principal's office. Ever again.

I don't want to get grounded in life
for always getting the wrong answer on the test.
I'm writing this down to be sure I remember.

The rule: Life is a test and you're screwed if you flunk.

A Special Blog Message From Will To The Reader

Dear Reader:

I always wanted to be Christopher Columbus. An adventurer, he sailed across the ocean and discovered a whole new land. He chose where he wanted to go and when he wanted to go there. He had *choices* and he knew how to follow his dreams.

Did you know that once upon a time the world was flat? Yes it was, because every father and every mother taught every child that was ever born that the world was flat. So that's just the way it was in the Land of Was.

Did you know that once upon a time we couldn't fly and no one had ever gone to the moon? People said, "If God wanted us to fly, He would have given us wings." But the Wright Brothers, President Kennedy, and Martin Luther King, Jr. refused to believe that the world was flat. The world is different because they had a dream.

That's what I want to do when I grow up; explore new things, go new places. I want my life to count and at my funeral people will stand up and say, "Will was the master of his own great ship, just like Christopher Columbus."

I need to wait until I'm older and in charge of my own life because trying to be a great adventurer now only gets me in trouble. In fact, I'm writing this in my journal to remind me to stop acting like Christopher Columbus. This is the Land of Was and thinking like that gets me sent to the principal's office. And that gets me grounded.

Will Remember. Will Remember. Will Remember.

Here's what happened. We took this test, and the first question was:

Is the world (A) flat, (B) round, or (C) maybe? A multiple choice test gives me choices. I almost marked flat because in the Land of Was it sure felt flat to me. I don't see people venturing off to new places or doing new things.

Martin Luther King, Jr. got killed for thinking in a new direction. I'm lucky I just got grounded because in the Land of Was everyone stays around and does what their dad and their grandpa did, sort of thinking the same old things. The only time we do something new is when we buy something new. On the test, I thought about it and checked 'maybe.'

The teacher marked my answer wrong. When I tried to explain that the world in Was is maybe kind of flat, she got upset. Teachers tell us to think outside the box but I guess they don't *mean* to really think outside their box.

Next she says, "If you don't pay attention and get better grades, you won't get a good job when you grow up."

So I said, "Good job is an oxymoron and it's great I can't get one because I'm never going to get a job." I'm not going to be a stuffy lawyer like my dad or a stuffy banker like my uncle. I'm going to be an entrepreneur and start a company just like Bill Gates and be rich and famous and have my life be a great adventure like Christopher Columbus. I want my life to be significant. I want to make a *difference*.

My teacher said, "Well, Mr. Strong Will with a smart mouth, let's just go to the principal's office and straighten out your thinking." The principal called my parents.

Dear Reader,
You can take my word as gospel about this!!
You DO NOT ever (and I mean never) want your
parents to get a call to come to the principal's office.

First, I got a long lecture from the principal about my attitude. Then, I got a lecture from my parents. I got in more trouble because I told them all the truth. "You grownups aren't happy working in your J.O.B. which means "just over broke." They pay you just enough so that you can't afford to quit, but not enough to be financially secure and get out of the rat race."

The next thing I knew, I found myself grounded.

I tried one more time to talk to my parents about how I felt living in Was. I pleaded that I had talent and wanted to develop skills so I could have a life worth living. I told them, "I am a powerful, passionate, creative, leader who wants to make a difference in the world."

No one would listen In the end, I had to say that I thought the world was round. And I also had to say that I would listen more to get better grades so that I could one day get a good job.

Maybe there is something wrong with me. The teachers said I have attention deficit disorder and recommended medication. Do the drugs, keep my mouth shut, and don't make any more test mistakes. I'll take the drugs. Then, I'll fit in. Then, I'll get the job they want. Then, I'll have more. I'll be better. Things will be different.

But before I take the bitter medicine and get normal, I want to write it down one time and remember:

There was a time before I settled for less.
A time before I fit in and became mediocre.
A time in my youth when I had a dream.
A dream that life could be
an adventure for everyone.
A dream that creative thinking
isn't the same thing as attention deficit disorder.
A dream that I matter because I am born.

Questions:

1. What were you taught about honesty as a child? What conflicting messages did you get? (e.g. " if you don't have something nice to say, don't say anything at all.")

2. List three examples where you were told to conform. What were the consequences if you did not?

A Note from Pure Joy to the Reader About School

Dear Reader,

Going to school in the Land of Was is going to be a blast. There are lots of people to talk to and they are all different colors, races, shapes, and sizes. I have so many new kids to play with and I intend to make friends with every single person in my school.

My friend, Will, is in my grade. He pretends to be a famous explorer, sailing the ocean. He is so daring. That's when I discovered that maybe school won't be such a blast after all, because we aren't just learning that 2 + 2 = 4. We are also learning the rules about living in the Land of Was. Will learned about the rules the hard way when he got sent to the principal's office. The teacher called him, Mr. Strong Stubborn Will and she said, "I've just about lost my patience with you, young man. You need to learn some manners." Then he got grounded. That's when I got clear that some of the rules are written but some are unspoken. That's when I started to learn how confusing life can be. "They" just have so many rules, it's hard to keep it all straight. I want to be good and I want to do well in school but, yikes, how does anyone keep all these rules straight?

Who are "THEY," you ask?
"They" are the people who write the rules
in the Land of Was.

I don't know their names but they teach us
when we can talk
and when children can be seen and not heard.
Those times when we can play
but only with kids who live on the right side of town.

To be careful because it's a jungle out there.
That people are waiting to take advantage of us
because we're not smart enough to know who to trust.

They teach us how smart we are and how smart we aren't.
That girls aren't good at math,
and boys communicate and think with their you-know-what.

All of the above teaches us
exactly how much money we'll make
if we ever grow up—which is doubtful.

Besides not being able to talk and share when I want to,
I'm also not allowed to explore certain
out-of-the-question ideas.
It's okay to learn certain politically correct things
(like not talking about who farts).
There are rules about how I must learn
a certain way.
Why?

Because that's how it's done in the Land of Was.

Sometimes I wish I could stay home and talk to Destiny all day. When they ask what illness I have, I'll say I'm sick and tired of going to school and being bored all day. I know Destiny isn't real. But once in awhile I forget that I'm not supposed to create Destiny. It's okay though because I don't try to create her that often anymore. I've learned that I have to go to school for the get-a-good-job part of the rules to work.

Or, because I'm a girl, I can grow up and get a good guy. He will handle the good-job part. I'll catch a guy and he can take care of everything.

In school I have to do all these things I don't want to do in ways I don't want to do them.

Take all the tests
and if I flunk the test, then I'm cooked.
But if I ace the test
the other kids hate me.
I have to
look good,
be right,
and be in control.
But, I hate it.

Internal Memo
From: Pure Joy
To: Pure Joy

On the subject of love and hate, I love to draw. People comment that my pictures are colorful. If my work has creative genius, why are they trying to improve on what I create? I want to paint by my own design, frame my works the way I want to, and hang the picture of life where I choose.

Why don't people create and improve their own stuff? If other people want to color only inside the lines I let them, but why do they tell me how to create my picture? It makes me angry that they have the right to tell me what works, what's missing, and what's next for my creation.

On the other hand, maybe they are right. Maybe I need to try harder to color the right way. But the right way is dull. Should I give up?

I know school is good. I call show and tell day, shareday. Tomorrow is not just sameday but a real share-myself-with-others-day. Sharing can be cosmic. Every moment should be a profound time to share myself with others.

I'm bringing a piece of beautiful wood I found in the forest. I'll wear my absolutely favorite outfit; my sunshine yellow carpenter coveralls. Those bright pants go with my hair and freckles. My toy hammer that is just like my dad's big hammer, fits in the loop on the side of the pants.

Tomorrow I expect to have a perfect day.

Questions:

1. What memories did this section trigger for you?

2. From what occurred, what decisions did you make about yourself and how you should live?

From the Locked and Sacred Diary of P.J.

These are my private thoughts.
Don't you dare look inside or read
on threat of extreme consequences.
Ignorance is bliss—and that's a rule.
P.J.

Dear Diary,

I can't figure out what's wrong with me. I love to share myself, my lunch snacks, and my ideas about how life is an adventure. I thought I was magical. I thought I was cute in my outfit today on shareday. But the kids made fun of my name and of me.

Fatty Fatty, two by four	*(They sang)*
Can't fit through the kitchen door.	*(They rhymed)*
Why, you ask: too much jelly	*(Oh, my gosh)*
Went right to her big fat belly.	*(Ouch!)*
It's peanut butter every day	*(Oh, my)*
So now we call her Miss P.J.	*(I'm not P.J.)*

P is for peanut butter, J is for jelly,
Since Miss Pure Joy likes it,
Let's call her P.J.

Oh, what fun we made of my name. I made fun of it, too. I joined in because, well, it was sort of funny (in a sinking feeling kind of way).

Later in the girls bathroom, I heard someone whisper that I thought I was going to be a builder like my dad but the only two by four I had was a big two by four butt. "She thinks she's so-o-o-o-o smart."

Other girls whispered and laughed. I'm sure it was about me. I wish my Destiny was here to talk to, but I don't see my Destiny anymore.

Something has to be wrong with me, otherwise why don't I fit in? Why do I have all these ugly parts about me? Why? So my friends have something to laugh at, that's why? What were my parents thinking when they named me Pure Joy? There's no sense talking to my parents because they are almost 40. Everybody knows the rule that life is over at 40.

In the Land of Was, people don't understand about Pure Joy. A few people started calling me P.J. for short. I hate it, I hate it, I hate it!

Maybe they're right. So what if I'm not Pure Joy anymore.

P.J. is short.

P.J. is easy for people to remember.

It's a normal sort of name.

I'll settle for normal and then I'll fit in.

Maybe I just imagined I could be Pure Joy. Most dreams can't come true anyway. As a matter of fact in Was, I've never seen a dream come true.

Maybe I am too fat. I'll find a way to lose ten pounds by next week.

When I'm thin, I'll fit in.
When I'm like the normal people, then I'll be okay.
What a great affirmation!
Much better than Pure Joy is who I am.

The next step of my plan to fit in is that I'll stop answering the teacher's questions. I don't need to be little miss yellow coveralls 'A' student.

One more thing. My pictures are bigger than life and I use every color of the rainbow to capture magic on paper. But I will never again color outside the lines. Coloring outside the lines is not normal.

Soooooooo, mirror, mirror on the wall.
This is who I am.
I am a thin, trim P.J.
who analyzes and edits what I will share and say
and knows how to be a perfect,
color-inside-the-lines sort of girl.

When I grow up, I'll get a normal job
and work hard
and marry the right, normal guy
and have exactly two kids
and the perfect house with a white picket fence
and then it will be my turn.
Everyone will come to my parties
and I'll get invited to the best parties.

My life is planned and settled. From here on I don't have to worry about it anymore. I will stay inside the perfect box.

Questions:

1. What are your rewards for fitting in?

2. What are your prices for fitting in?

3. What are your rewards for being authentic and true to yourself?

4. What are the prices you pay for fitting into the normal box?

They Took My Picture, I've Been Framed

Internal Memo
From: P.J.
To: P.J.

There are big decisions to make and I need to make the right decision. My life depends on it. It's not about what I want. Everybody knows the rule; life is a compromise.

This week we are going to the photography studio to take a family photo. The photographer is beautiful and elegant. When she takes pictures she laughs and everybody says cheese.

What's the rub?

What to wear!

Of all my outfits, my yellow coveralls is the best outfit for me to be exactly me in the picture. My bright pants, white patent leather shoes, and white socks with yellow lace trim.

My dad bought that outfit and they are a copy of his coveralls. When we go to the lumber store and places around town, everybody smiles and says I'm cute. My dad beams and he is so proud that he puffs out his chest and the buttons almost pop off his shirt.

I wore that outfit when we took a photo to advertise my dad's business. People naturally recognize me in this exact outfit. There I am in the newspaper, wearing my coveralls with my toy hammer and a big board working on the job site right next to my Daddy. Below my picture it says, "Build it with brick, Daddy, build it with brick."

But everyone knows that only red dresses or green dresses with lace are allowed in Christmas pictures. People wear white shoes between Easter and Labor Day. But Christmas is after Labor Day and after Labor Day you should only wear black shoes. If I break this rule I will be on the worst dressed list and a social outcast for at least one year, two months, and four hours.

I guess I'll wear the red satin dress hanging in my closet waiting for this picture occasion.

From the Locked Diary of P.J.

These are my private and personal thoughts. Read on if you must. I don't care much anymore. How I feel isn't all that important anyway, is it?

Get over it and grow up because big girls don't cry. This may not be a rule but it's a song which can be the same as a rule.

P.J.

Dear Diary,

Look there's no sense in crying over this thing,
so I'm keeping it short.
We got the pictures back.
I was so excited.
When I locked,
there was a sweet, pretty girl
but the girl wasn't me.

Dear Diary,
I asked my mom and dad,
"Who is this person in our family portrait?
Where am I?
I seem to be lost,
because the girl in this portrait isn't me!"

They didn't understand a thing I was talking about.
My mom took my temperature
to see if I was sick or 'lucinating
or whatever you call the disease when you're nuts.

I wonder sometimes if I'm normal...

One thing was nice,
the picture was beautifully framed.

Question:

1. Give two examples when you "played a part" but didn't feel you were yourself.

2. Your life may be framed beautifully on the outside. To others it looks beautiful…but if it could look exactly the way you wanted the picture to look, how would it look?

3. Can you remember a time in your life when you were the artist painting on the canvas of your life?

A Note From The Author

To: The Reader
Regarding: Kids Grow Up

Twenty years have passed.
Will and P.J. were childhood friends.
Then they were childhood sweethearts.
They grew up and married each other.

They have jobs, a house, kids, and a dog.

FAST FORWARD YOUR MIND.

Beware —

You are about to enter the adult world in the Land of Was

Life Drifts On in the Land of Was

Internal Memo
From: Will
To: Will

That Gawd-awful noise cannot
(please—it ***cannot****)*
be the alarm clock already.
I'll just push the snooze for five more minutes.
I'm so tired.
I went to bed early.
I got plenty of sleep.
So why, oh, why am I always so tired?

Darn, there it goes again,
jarring-revolting-snapping-intruding.
Yanking me out of my warm, peaceful sleep.
Is it a Saturday or Sunday?
No. Drat!
That means it's another Sameday.

Tick, tock. Tick, tock. Same-day. Same-day.
When will it be ***my*** *day?*

It would be nice to sleep in, to get peace and rest, have time to renew, relax, and nurture my spirit. But there goes that clock again. ***Tick, tock. Tick, tock****. It's easy for Wayne Dyer, living the life in Hawaii, to meditate everyday and write books about* The Power Of Intention. *He's not in this rat race. He doesn't understand how it is in the real Was world.*

I'm not complaining—I have a nice job.
But it's still a job.
It owns me,
not the other way around.
I started out to make a difference;
in the company—
for my family—
in the world.
My life Was supposed to be
a Magical Journey of Adventure,
and I Was supposed to make a big contribution in life.
What happened?

How does a person go from the hopes and dreams of youth to this dead-end alarm clock that controls time and keeps me stuck in the Land of Was? How did I start out being me and end up like ***this****? How did my life end up in this dead-end, this-is-the-way-it's-always-been Land of Was existence where one day of sameness drifts to the next?*

Okay, it's time to get my act together.
Stumble out of bed,
hit the shower, dress.
Orange juice with bacon and eggs sounds great.
But, Will, look at that clock. Get a move on old man.
No time for breakfast.
Grab a doughnut from the kitchen
and stop for a cup of java on the way.

I'm proud of our house. Look at this gourmet kitchen. P.J. did an awesome job with the décor. Even in school, she had this knack for color and design. It was a smart move the day I married her. And man, not only does she know color, she also throws an awesome party. Everyone wants to come to our parties. Sometimes I forget what an incredible woman P.J. is. Will, my man, you definitely have an awesome wife.

Of course, the romance isn't the zany trip it used to be.
It was hot, hot, hot in the early days.
But in the here and now, it's more than a little stale.
Now that new girl at the office,
there's one sexy dish.
With her things wouldn't be stale.
Probably take me two or three days to recover.

Hey, what's wrong with you,
thinking junk like that?
It's not worthy of you.

HELLO THERE?
!!! WILL !!!
THIS IS YOUR CONSCIENCE CALLING!!!

It's a good thing I'm in the back recesses of your mind
to remind you what a piece of crud you are.
You are shameful. One nasty, despicable dude.

Well, it's not like I'm touching. The rule clearly states that I can look but can't touch. What harm is there in looking? It's not like P.J. will ever know what I'm thinking. Some things are best not to talk about, ***especially*** *with your wife.*

I don't know why I think crazy off-the-wall things. No wonder my wife can't get turned on anymore.

I'm not sure I deserve the good life I have. Sure, I live in a great house. Sure, I've got two great kids who get good grades and who only have to be asked two or three times to set the table. But if everything is so great, then why am I feeling run down and depressed and so gosh dang tired? Why do I have thoughts I know won't support my marriage?

What's wrong with me?
I'm doing exactly what I need to be doing
to have the right stuff
that everyone wants in the Land of Was.

Everyone in the neighborhood must want to be just like me.
If I have all the right stuff, though,
why are my golf clubs buried
somewhere in the garage,
getting rusty?

Why haven't I taken a hike in the woods
or gone fishing with my kids
in who knows how long?

Oh, well—no time to think about these things now.

I have a j-o-b to go to. A man has to make sacrifices to climb that ladder of success. If I have to step on someone else's fingers to reach the next rung of the ladder, well, that's the way it is in the Land of Was. They would have stepped on my fingers first chance they got. It's nothing personal. Strictly business.

Everyone is somewhere on the ladder.
Either above me or below me.
My job is to get my head above the next person.
That's how the business world works.
I didn't make these rules,
I just live by them.

When they made the rules, they should have asked me.
But they didn't, so there's nothing I can do about it.
I'm the victim.
The same as the next poor sap, who is climbing the ladder
to get my spot.

*It's always been like that and always **will** be like that*
in the Land of Was.

Questions:

1. What is a specific area of your life where you feel trapped—you interpret it as have-to or an obligation?

2. What is an alternate way to interpret the same situation which will create joy and excitement?

Money Doesn't Grow on Trees

Note taped to the trash can:

From: P.J.
To: Will

Dear Will,

Don't you know that it isn't our lot in life to have abundance financially? So why are you climbing that ladder? Looking for money up that tree?

I love you.
I see how hard you try,
but it is futile.
We aren't the Rockefellers, you know.
As hard as you try, you should realize
that money doesn't grow on trees.

The proof is that we are always broke. We don't have much, but we'll get by. What you do everyday at work may not make much difference, but it's okay that we settled for normal because money isn't everything.

Hugs and kisses,

P.J.

P.S. Maybe we can have a romantic evening tonight? Please stop by the grocery on your way home and pick up a bottle of wine. Some flowers would be nice. Of course, since I had to remind you that I want them it won't mean as much that you get them. You can still try once in a while. I love you very, very much.

Huhhhhh?

Internal Memo
From: Will
To: Will

What's with P.J. leaving notes taped to the trash can?
Does she want to have sex?
Or
does she want to criticize?
Is this a not-so-subtle hint for me to take out the trash?
She doesn't appreciate me.
I work hard—I do more than my share.
Screw her.
Screw the flowers.
I don't have time for this drama.
It's time to get to work – work – work.

Questions:

1. What is a specific situation where you've had a completely different experience than the other person involved—and you felt you were completely misunderstood?

2. Write about the incident as if you were in their shoes instead of yours.
   What actions did you take?
   What actions did they take?

3. Now!! Pretend you have no control over what they did or said—rather pretend that you alone could have changed things to produce a different outcome. Hint: Start with a way of being. (example: I could have been vulnerable, powerful, loving, forgiving, understanding etc.)

4. Would you have to give up a belief system about the situation? Would you have to give up "being right" about your point of view regarding the situation?

5. What way of being and actions could you have taken to produce a different outcome?

6. Here's the key question!!!! What action can I take right now to powerfully influence the situation to a positive outcome?

Driving My Life Away

Internal Memo
From: Will
To: Will

Ah, there's my new baby, my shiny new car. I can't wait to drive around town today with the top down, smelling that new-car smell. Of course, the car is three months old now, so that new-car smell is wearing off. Nor does it make much sense to put the top down in winter. If I do put the top down, how will I look by the time I get to the office? Will can't look a mess.

To climb the ladder of success I must, I must, I must
always look good,
be right,
and be in total control.

I did enjoy the impression the new car made that first few days when I pulled into my parking spot at work.

When I ***have*** nice stuff,
I'll ***do*** the things rich people do,
(like drive with the top down,)
and then I'll ***be*** happy.
As soon as I have more,
life will be better
and things will *be* ***different.***

More = Better = Different
That's the way it is in Was.

I might have to look for something new again.
I might stop by the car dealer after work
and see what they have.
I wonder what kind of trade in they'll take on this car?
It's practically brand new.

Ah, here comes a Starbucks. I can hit the drive-through, thank goodness for convenience. Why wait in line with the other schmucks, when I can sit in my car and pick up my $4.00 cup of special brew latte while listening to tunes on my iPod?

They're playing my song.
I can't get no satisfaction.
Well I try and I try and I try and I try.
I can't get no, no satisfaction.

Finally, some caffeine. Who needs breakfast with Starbucks nearby? Traffic is heavy. Are those church bells? This isn't Sunday, a day to relax and rejoice. This is a sameday and everyone in the Land of Was knows that samedays are for work and hurry and bustle and getting things done. It must be a funeral or maybe a wedding. Like there's a difference. Weddings and funerals look the same to me.

I have caffeine and my cell phone, only a few exits from work. If I find parking close to the entrance, I might not even be late.

Look out Land of Was,
there are deals to be made
and work to be done
and 'ole Will is just about in the house.

Questions:

1. Give an example when you got something you thought would make you happy, but it didn't work or wore off quickly.

Have, Do, and Be Rule

Internal Memo
From: Will
To: Will

Today, my job is to work hard,
do the right things,
then everything will be okay.
As soon as I'm doing enough,
and if I do the right thing exactly the right way,
then me and mine will
have the good stuff.
Then, and only then,
I'll be happy.
I'll be stress-free.
I'll be powerful.
I'll be cool.

I'll be who I always dreamed I could be!
And if that formula doesn't work,
then I obviously did something wrong.

As soon as I have
the right job,
the right house,
the perfect wife,
then I'll do the things successful people do.

And then and only then I'll be
happy, powerful, complete, and whole.

Questions:

1. Pretend that you are on your deathbed looking back at your life. Has "Have-Then Do-Then Be" ever worked in your life?

   You aren't dead yet 'cause you're reading this book and dead people can't read—so guess what it's not too late!!

How are you changing right now?
Your thoughts are different right now—in this right now moment.
You are not who you were 5 minutes ago!!
Sooooooooo, not someday in the future but RIGHT NOW
How are you changing (changed) RIGHT NOW?
WHAT ACTION CAN YOU TAKE RIGHT NOW
TO CHANGE A SITUATION—TO CHANGE YOUR LIFE
RIGHT NOW?

START BEING THAT PERSON
TAKE THAT ACTION
WHEN?
RIGHT NOW!!!

Life in the Day of Survivor

Internal Memo
From: Will
To: Will

Is it 5:00 p.m. yet? What? Only 10:00 a.m.?

Another day, another couple of dollars, another attempt at climbing up that big, old corporate ladder. They need to pay me more. Just about everyone is out to get me, steal my market share, and take the credit for the work I did. People hate me when all I'm doing is my job.

There's so much to do. There's the report, the e-mail inbox is about to overflow, and there are messages on my cell phone. Gotta read this report. That number is off, which makes the whole chart invalid. How sloppy, people. This is business. Things have to be ***perfect****.*

Wait a second—this is Sadie's report. She thinks she'll waltz in and take my designated tenured place on the ladder? It's not my job to get involved in her department. If she wants to run with the big dogs, she'd better learn to take it on the chin. I've got too much on my plate as it is to be trying to help someone else. If she gets knocked down a notch, that means I go up. That's the way it works in the Land of Was. I win when someone else loses. Just like checkers. You're either the red or the black. I know it sounds harsh, but I didn't make the rules. I just live by them.

What time is it now? 11:15 a.m. Is that all?

Time to turn in the report. The stuff is going to hit the fan when they see the mistake on her chart, and the notes I added on. This is business, and the worse the Sadies of the world look, the better for me and mine.

Hey, Sadie, Sadie Sexy Lady, how's that nice corner office? Nice corner spot, right by the water cooler. A person with that office could slip in late and no one would know. Come to think of it, I don't remember seeing Sadie on time lately. I haven't seen her late, either but maybe she's been slipping in late all this time. Here I am, hustling, trying to get ahead, and there are people coming in late all the time. It would serve her right to catch heck for messing up the numbers in that chart, and coming in late.

If everyone in the office was as dedicated as me, things would be a lot better. Sales would be up. Morale would be up. How much longer can I carry all these slackers?

I need to be busy when they call from upstairs on that report. I'll get e-mails answered and go to lunch. This afternoon's meeting, which is useless, will take up most of my time. Then I'm blowing out of here. If I play it right, I can stop for a drink or three, hightail it home, dish up a plate of whatever the wife throws my way, and settle back with my TV tray in time to watch the next episode of Survivor.

Questions:

1. Where do you feel victimized in your life? Two specific examples. (e.g. my in-laws try to sabotage my marriage)

2. What is an area in life where you play the game called "for me to win someone else must lose"?

3. Who is someone you resent? How come?

The Romance is Gone From His Marriage in Two Years

Internal Memo
From: Will
To: Will

I cannot understand why P.J. is fixated on her weight. I married her, didn't I? And what's up with that note she sent me? Money doesn't grow on trees. She could show a little appreciation for how hard I work to provide the good things in life for our family.

Tonight I'm going to sit back with a cold bottle of beer and watch TV.

I'll turn off my brain, go to oblivion,
and forget about the rat race for a few hours.
I love her and she loves me,
so I shouldn't get all bent out of shape about the small stuff.
I sure don't understand women!

The Romance is Gone From Her Marriage in Two Years

Internal Memo
From P.J.
To: P.J.

No need to fuss over dinner. Fix macaroni and cheese, green beans, and fried pork chops.

I don't understand Will. He says we don't have sex often enough? So I sent him a note to say tonight is our night and all he cares about is watching television. Why won't he try? Why isn't he romantic anymore?

He probably thinks I'm fat. He doesn't want me anymore. If he doesn't care then there's no sense for me to try either.

I'll make potatoes and gravy with the pork chops.

I sure don't understand men!

Questions:

1. What do you think about a specific relationship/person and you haven't told them?

2. What are the rewards and prices for NOT communicating?

3. What do you imagine would be the rewards/prices if you did communicate?

ATM Connection

Internal Memo:
From P.J.
To: Pure Joy

I'm bored
with everything
in the Land of Was.
I rush from here to there,
and here to work,
and here to wherever.
In the midst of the boring rushing,
I want to connect with a human being.

Since I'm going to the bank anyway,
I'll pick flowers from my garden
for the bank tellers.
That should break the boredom (theirs and mine)
and create a human connection.

Here I am standing in line,
with a bouquet of gorgeous flowers.
This line is long,
and
the kids will be home from school soon,
and
I haven't made it to the grocery,
and
my car is running on empty.
If I don't get out of this bank soon
I'll hit rush hour traffic.
I'd better just use the ATM machine.

Where's my ATM card?
My code. My code.
Press enter.

Hello, P.J. Welcome to the bank
Thank you for putting your trust in our system.

This machine is talking to me.

The ATM machine does not have eternal happiness stored inside its system.

ATM machines are not people.
There is no connection.
If the machine can talk to me,
then I'm talking back.

Effectively immediately my name is Pure Joy.

Dear Bank—You may know my credit score.

Dear ATM Machine—
You may know my bank account number,
And how many zeros I have in my account balance.
But!!! ***You don't know me!***
Let me repeat!!! You don't know me!

I am not hard wired—because I'm not a machine.
I am an occurring, evolving
Pure Joy person

(or, at least, I used to be)
and
I am now ready to be Pure Joy again.

I name myself, and
how I name myself is how others define me.

Questions:

1. Pure Joy said, "How I name myself is how others define me." How do you want to define yourself from this moment on?

2. What's the value you get with human connection?

3. What's a random act of kindness you've done?
   What did you experience?
   Did you have an expectation of the response you got?
   (e.g. they should be thankful)

It's About Time

Internal Memo
From: Pure Joy
To: Pure Joy

Suddenly I hear a bell. Why is it chiming at 3:33 a.m. on a perfectly normal Sameday? Will is sleeping soundly. I'll slip out of bed and putter downstairs to make coffee.

Tick tock, tick tock, tick tock.

That old grandfather clock woke me.

Perhaps once I get moving I'll feel alive. Feel that my life has purpose other than the fact that someone needs to take out the trash. Maybe once I get moving I'll realize my life matters. Did I mistakenly discard my Destiny when I took out the trash? Everyday is like yesterday with all the invisible other yesterdays stretched from Was to eternity.

I have a good life. Some would say a great life.
There's nothing traumatic or dramatic going on.
It doesn't seem right to feel the way I feel.
Other people have real problems,
like how to feed their children.
Like dying of cancer.
Like living homeless.
Having been raped.

I wonder if my intentions could work for me
if I'm willing to get real right here, right now?
Today I want to play a childhood game called ***What If.***

What if *my feelings are in fact my feelings?*
What if *I don't make them good or bad,*
right or wrong?

What if *I don't feel guilty because I'm not in crisis?*

What if *I can be internally honest*
about what's important to me?

What if *it really isn't all that painful to peek*
inside the locked suitcase of my truest desires?

What if *my Destiny is there waiting for me?*
Not lost, not set out on the curb with the trash,
but merely misplaced.
Waiting for the clock to strike this moment.

What if *this is the moment that I am ready*
to listen to, and follow,
the Destiny I locked away as a child?

What if *I don't need to be a certain Was way*
~ because today is not like yesterday, ~
~ Today is Today? ~

What if *I have a right to feel,*
but my feelings don't rule my life?

What if *I have the right to choose based on*
what I declare?
Based on what I am committed to?

What if *it is my birthright, honor, and privilege*
to set powerful and fulfilling intentions?

What if *I don't wait for my intention to show up in life?*

What if *I don't fret about how to make it happen?*

What if *I trust myself that the right actions will occur to me*
so that I can have whatever I am committed to?

What if *it's not airy-fairy to declare world peace?*

What if *world peace begins in my own family?*

What if *I quit driving my car by looking*
in the rearview mirror?

What if *I am willing to experience all that simply is?*

What if *I am the creator of the game of my life?*

***What if** life is both more and less than I can imagine,
and the more or less is in direct proportion to
the contribution I declare myself to be?*

***This changes everything.
It's exciting! I love my life!
It's time we move to the Land of Becoming.***

Questions:

1. Reread this section. Ask each "What if" question of yourself. Notice your immediate responses—no censoring! Write down any you consider significant.

Lost and Found

Up, up, up,
under the eaves of the attic,
in deep forgotten recesses,
buried under years of cobwebs,
lie the remaining embers
of hopes, dreams, and plans
which can live on
if only she can find them
inside the dusty diary of her mind.

From the Dusty Diary of Pure Joy

Dear Diary,

It's been so long since I wrote upon your pages.

I have a longing to move to the Land of Becoming. Just thinking about moving forward, of turning things around and uprooting my life, is daunting. I've wasted time worrying about how, and when, and where to start. The beginning of change is hard.

I need tools to guide me. Despite my fear, I'm moving forward in my life journey. There will be obstacles I must navigate over, under, around, or through.

Dear Diary,

For years, I've been driving the vehicle of my life
without headlights.
I didn't want to turn on the headlights,
I didn't want to look.
I thought that if I shut away my awareness and light,
I could pretend that drifting along was what I wanted.
It's a miracle that I have done as well as I have.
It's time to give myself self-acceptance.
I am proud of myself.
I have proven that I am powerful beyond belief.
If I've gotten this far while driving
from the backseat of my life,
imagine my future potential
because from this moment forward,
I'm aware of the immense value of
becoming a master at driving my life from the front seat
with my headlights on.

A steady flashlight will help me look at my map.
To drive out of the darkness,
I need powerful headlights.
High beams give me a
long-range, positive view of life's road.
Low beams help me focus
on things that block my path.
Bright headlights give me
courage to drive my life in the direction I choose.

For the first time in years
I believe that I can travel the distance
and have my intentions happen.
I have faith that I am.
Life is safe and full of adventure.
My family is safe
because I can show my kids how to drive out of the night.
The world is safe because as I master the art
of driving with headlights, so will others.
Together we can create
a powerful light for all of humanity.
Imagine how bright the world is becoming
as we reach a critical mass
of everyone driving
with their lights on.

Questions:

1. What are you proud of thus far in your life's journey? List 3 specific instances.

2. With your headlights on, what do you imagine would be different with your experience of life?

3. What personal growth work are you willing to do in order to have your deepest commitments and intentions show up powerfully in your life?.

Remember Who You Are

For Pure Joy To Be In Search of Free Will
She must first remember who she is!!!

Will?
Will?
I love you!
I love you!
I love you!
Where are you?
I know I'm shouting throughout the house
in Pure Joy,
looking for you.

I'm shouting in sheer Pure Joy
Because I've found myself,
Come Home To Myself!

NOW!! I'm ready for the rambunctious adventure
of searching for you because
I'm not interested in connecting
with ATM machines anymore.
I'm not connecting with
how much money we have anymore.
Don't get me wrong!!
I'm cool if we have a great big bunch of abundance
BUT it doesn't define me
AND
It's not who I am.

I'm done with the maze of thinking all inside my head.
I want to have a real conversation
with the real you
and the real me.

I don't know what makes today different than yesterday.
But I know that it's time
for us to move to the Land of Becoming.
Isn't knowing that it's time to move forward a
wondrous miracle?
I found my precious little doll from my childhood
that I forgot about and shut away.
It's time to free our destinies,
regardless of where or why we
locked them away.

Life is a miracle.
You are a miracle.
Our life together is a miracle.
In the ups and the downs,
the ins and outs,
life remains a miracle.
I am an integral part of the glory of it all
because I am the miracle named Pure Joy.

Remember Who You Are!!

Free Will Can't Have A Meaningful Marriage With Pure Joy Until He First Remembers That
He Is FREE WILL

P.J.?

Joy?

Pure Joy!

I love you too.

I love you to the moon and back.

I love you in this moment and beyond.

I'm sitting up in this oak tree
but not to hide.
I came here to think.
I like to be outside,
in the wide open spaces,
at sunrise
before all the seemingly important
somethings intrude and
I'm the have-no-choices,
struggle-through-the-day-guy
I have become.

It's About Now!
Deciding the Future Based on Commitment

My dearest Free Will—Somehow I forgot that I AM Pure Joy,
So it was natural to then forget that you are my Free Will.
All these years we've been married
I thought you climbed this tree
to get away from me.
I have misinterpreted
that part of our marriage.

I may be interpreting a lot of my life
from my belief that I'm not lovable.

My outdated belief that I don't know how to dress,
and look right, so I must not be lovable.
(Right?)
(Wrong!)

Back in school,
I thought girls were laughing at me.
And, out of the belief that they were laughing,
somewhere inside
I made a decision that said,
"Pure Joy you aren't lovable."
From that day and every sameday after that
I believed
that unless I looked a certain way,
and performed in bed a certain way,
then no one will love me.

I don't even know if they were whispering about me.
AND SO WHAT if they were?
It Was twenty years ago.
We were all just kids.
How could
some long ago whisper
affect whether
I'm Pure Joy?

Over the years,
I've gathered evidence
to prove that I'm not worthy of love.
So my Dear Free Will
Every time you climb this tree,
I used it as proof that
you wish you could leave me
because I'm not worth being around.
When I leave you notes
about climbing ladders,
I'm actually jealous of an old oak tree.

Regardless of obstacles and barriers from my past
insecurities that I'm not good enough,

I know for sure
I truly love you.
In this moment I re-affirm
my commitment to this love.
I am yours and you are mine.

Together we decide what our future will bring.
There is no way on no day that I want to separate Pure Joy
and Free Will in my life.
I am not the past.
I am not the future.
I am the Pure Joy
I bring to my life and our union
in this moment.

My dearest Pure Joy,
You are the
wonderful
creative
loving
silly minx
who stole my heart,
the day you wore
those yellow coveralls
to class in fourth grade.

I fell in love with you because
you love to share of yourself.
You were willing to be
in the moment of Pure Joy.
When you felt like it was a yellow coverall day
the room filled with sunshine.
You are my fashion trend.

Once upon a time,
in the flat and barren Land of Was
I fell in love with this
spontaneous,
light hearted,
confident and loved–to-share–of-herself
Pure Joy woman girl,
I see right here—right now.

Pure Joy,
I wanted to be your
daring,
dashing,
adventurous
knight in shining armor.

Yet the armor I wear trying to protect you and my
family became so heavy that it wore me down.

The armor is so rusty I'm afraid to
climb down the ladder.

It's so hot in my armor,
it makes me weary to my soul.

Yet I have felt deep within,
that Pure Joy is there,
and Pure Joy will bring me home to myself.
Pure Joy is right here waiting,
assuring me that I can put away the armor.

I desire to be daring,
but I need to know that I am enough,
just as I AM,
with no armor between me and the ones I love.

I've forgotten how to
let loose of the armor,
let loose of the grind,
and simply wrap my arms around you.
Wrap my arms around my joyous life.

I want to be the father and husband
who makes you proud.

It's so long since I felt anything under this armor that
I forgot I have feelings.
Talking to you today
I see clearly,
I feel wholly
I AM Free Will.

From my own Free Will self
I love you.

I AM the knight of the realm I declare for my life.
I am the Knight of Pure Joy.
Let us mark this day not as any sameday.

I do proclaim this day, this time, this place,
to be the Land of Becoming.

I do not need outdated armor.
In the Land of Becoming I do not need to be
encased in any fixed way of being.

For I am created out of nothing.
I AM no thing.
I AM no fixed,
have-to-be-a-certain-way, Being.

I cannot create myself to be
"I am"
out of what I have become.
That Was me
but it isn't me now.

I can only create the Free Will me
out of the possibility
I am.

I stand naked and vulnerable before you.
I am your Free Will.

We will have happy times,
and sad times,
and the oh, so boring times,
and glorious times,

every step of the journey is our Destiny's path.

Life is an adventure
in the Land of Becoming.

Today is a renewal of the
marriage between
Free Will and Pure Joy.

Questions:

1. List 3 examples of negative self-talk that keeps you stuck in WAS.

2. Write 3 positive affirmations that replace the negating phrases.

3. Who do you want to have a real conversation with? What do you appreciate about this person?.

____

____

____

____

____

____

____

____

____

____

____

____

____

But What Happened Then?

That's pretty much the story. You might be wondering whatever became of Pure Joy and Free Will. Who are they now? Where are they? Are they on a journey of transformation?

These questions are not as simple to answer as you may think for I am, and you are, Pure Joy and Free Will. This story is about the inner child in each of us. The story of your life isn't complete. Nor is mine. We are still Becoming.

I am more than a fantasy, but never dare to think of me as a certainty. I live as a possibility. I use my work (whatever I do) as a basic structure to create my possibilities into certainty. I am still Becoming.

I'm the girl who hadn't filed tax returns for seven years prior to the day I walked into a workshop. I had such a burning desire to have things different in my life that I pawned my wedding ring and sold my refrigerator to pay for an advanced course. I believed that change was possible for me. I walked into the IRS after that course, shaking in my shoes, because I didn't have a clue how I'd pay the $90,000 I owed.

I'm the frightened girl who didn't believe she could support herself financially when I was divorced and broke after 25 years of marriage. Today, I'm the kid who owes the IRS nothing and I'm part of the top five percent of wage earners in the United States. All because I know how to change and grow and become a committed, powerful me. I am a pioneer in the work of creating a world I envision as harmonious and loving.

In the past I painted myself so small that my life and the life of my family suffered. I am also a person who uses the results that don't work in my life to create urgency so that I am responsible that it doesn't happen again. I've enrolled thousands to begin life anew, encouraging each to see a better vision for their own life. A father called his 15 year old daughter that he hadn't spoken to in five years because I'm eager to make a difference in the lives of my students.

I am a sixty-something-year-old grandmother who vows to make a positive difference in my own family. I am a wondrous, cosmic being who declares that my life matters, and I prove that statement true moment by moment in an ever occurring, ever changing world. I create community in this everyday, occurring world. The world is going to be better because I say so. In spite of what I don't do perfect, the Becoming me makes a difference. A difference last week, this week, and next week because it occurs to me to declare it as so.

I reveal myself, I listen, I talk and report, I authentically and generously share my gifts.

Each of us was born to live in the Land of the Becoming. It is my heritage and our birthright to "become." Who I am, who I create myself to be, and what tools I use to create the unique me that "I am," is not as important as the fact that it occurs to me to promise, declare, inspire, and request support. I am a powerful, passionate, creative, loving, leader. I am a person of my word, and being a person of my word, I promise that whatever I am creating myself to be, that beingness will be an invitation and will support my dream and my stand.

To create a world where children from every background are born into, a world which fosters an internal knowledge of their unique value, yet generates and celebrates their connection to the global community.

Join me in having a life worth living. As you design and invent your life to be abundant, joyous, and full of contribution, it creates an invitation for others to follow your lead. Join me as we create a world that works for all human kind.

Questions:

1. What, for you, is a Life Worth Living? Write one page in detail, giving yourself complete permission.

2. What kind of person (specific qualities) would you need to be to create that life?.

PART II

PRESENTS A ROADMAP TO GUIDE YOU IN LIVING THE LIFE OF YOUR DREAMS NOW!

HOW TO USE THE FOLLOWING SECTIONS OF THE BOOK TO YOUR BEST ADVANTAGE

This section provides steps and ideas which guide us to live in the Land of Becoming. Each concept is simple on the surface. The challenge for each of us is to practice staying aware. The good news is that from now on, any time you feel stuck, lose your serenity, or forget to approach life as a brand new day, you will have tools you can use to shift into new practices that produce the experience and results you want. All you need to do is practice your chosen ways of being-doing-having.

Treat yourself gently. Living a transformed life requires that each of us stay attuned to our everyday, moment-to-moment awareness. There are still days when I end up back in my stuff, back in my own Land of Was. Progress is about how fast I catch myself living in Was and make a choice to move once again to the Land of Becoming.

Most of us have been taught about right and wrong. We are doing the best we know how to do. If we knew how to do life better, we would already be doing it. For my perfectionists out there DO NOT let the areas of your life that you are working on be about how "good" or "bad" you are doing. Don't allow the joy of learning and growing to turn into a conversation of "I'm not good enough" or "this isn't good enough."

The following reminders will support you in staying present to what you are up to.

Find a quiet moment each morning
and read the steps out loud
until they become a comfortable part of who you are.
You can visit Toniraye.com
And download the affirmations at no cost.

1) **For the next 30 days, I refuse to worry about whether I am doing things the right or wrong way. It is my intention to lay it all down and give it a rest for all areas of my life.** The life of our planet will change when each of us lays down our guilt around what is right and wrong, and live based on what works, what doesn't, and what's next.

2) **The philosophical view of using transformation as a way of life is not about "The Truth," like 1 +1 = 2.** It is about one possibility for me to access power and a life that works.

3) **Living a transformed life is my chosen truth for my life.** It is not a righteous tool used to judge others.

4) **As I understand the belief systems I have created, I have the power to transform my view of my life and the world around me. I am creating a new core set of beliefs which support my choices for life.**

5) **As I powerfully transform my thoughts, I always have an internal safe haven.** I am inventing a space—an inner place to ground to, and to come from, which empowers my life. This safe haven is where I return when I forget my power or momentarily lose the path I have set for myself. I am no longer a victim of other people or situations.

6) **Anytime I lose my sense of serenity, I stop and reground to a more powerful belief system.** I allow myself a moment to breathe and be aware that something around me is not in alignment with the results I have chosen for myself. With awareness, my internal wisdom will begin moving me once again toward serenity. I experience the freedom of choosing to be responsible.

7) **I Am a Becoming, evolving being who is not concerned about being perfect. I am delighted with the notion that I will never arrive because I am on my way to becoming a new me. I see this as part of the adventure of my life.**

   I am all right and the universe is here to help me.

   I am the perfect me in this perfect place, at this perfect time.

   I am whole and complete right where I am.

   As I surrender to the "me" that I am in this moment, it gives me the perfect opportunities to design myself

to any "me" I want to be.
Example: When I surrender and embrace that I am scared and doubting myself in this moment, I can then declare myself to be courageous.

8) **I have the capacity to create my life the way I say matters. I create close relationships, a fulfilling career, great health, contribution to the community—success in the areas of life that matter to me.**

9) **Even as I read and begin to internalize these affirmations my life is improving. My thoughts are now changed and can never return to old outdated ways of thinking.** I am no longer in the dark ages. I do not need to live in the Land of Was. I am a child born to live in the Land of Becoming.

Chapter 1

I Interpret, Therefore I Am

For me to realize that I have the power to create my life the way I decide, I must adopt a philosophy that life is an interpretation all the way to the core of who I am. Who are you? Who are you for the people in your life? How has your environment, the world culture, your ethnic culture, the kinds of jobs your parents had, shaped your view of yourself and the world around you? I was born; you were born, into a conversation. That conversation is both shouts and whispers. As human beings it can lift us up and beat us down. It is unwritten rules that shape us, mold us into who we are and what is possible for us to be. That already existing conversation tells us what is, and isn't, possible in our world. This conversation is most often about how to fit into an already existing framework of mediocrity.

> If I Want Unprecedented Powerful Results I Must Become A Master At Interpreting Powerfully.
> — toniraye

> How I Interpret Myself Determines The Quality Of My Life And The Quality Of The Contribution I Am.
> — toniraye

On the day of our birth, we were each a bright promise of the future. Little by little as we learned that 2 + 2 = 4, we misplaced the magic we were born to be. It didn't disappear all at once and it didn't disappear forever. It is lost in the daily grind of what we call life.

—toniraye

These words were first written as part of the *Escape From Was* introduction. I repeat them here because they are vital in understanding how we all have interpretations about life. Some of our interpretations work well for us as individuals and as a world culture. An example might be that life should be about contribution and commitment to what I say matters. But other interpretations may not work so well. Regardless of what kinds of interpretations we invent—our entire set of interpretations end up shaping what we believe, what we value as important or not in life. These interpretations often cause us to recklessly jump to unwarranted fixed belief systems. All of our results are then a direct product of the belief systems. The already existing conversation/interpretation drives our way of being, the choices we make in life, actions we take based on our choices, and the ensuing results that accumulate in our life and accrue forward to future generations. These fixed ideas take root and grow in each social culture, the country where you were born and raised, your ethnic origin, your gender, the type of education and job your parents had and the list goes on. These conversations and subsequent cultural beliefs change over time. However, due to the mass nature (sheer numbers) of people who believe the conversation/ interpretation "is true" it becomes difficult and sluggish to have the conversation change. After all, who are you to say what "the truth" is; you're not God or the leader of the entire world. Therefore, you may think that you have the authority or any possible way to change what useful modern thinking is or could be. Who are you to decide its ok to sit in the front of the bus? Who are you to create a new conversation called "world peace is possible"? Who are you to decide that a heart transplant will work thereby changing medical science forever? Who are you to decide we can put a man on the moon? Who are you to change the cultural conversation from spanking is necessary to my child can be raised to be an outstanding contributing human being without the need of corporal punishment? You are the person that interprets life in a way that makes it all possible or not...that's exactly who you are.

Alright already I get it—this kind of thick talk isn't every reader's cup of tea. Using an example I touched on during the story when Will was sent to the principal's office might help me explain and lighten the mood here.

Once upon a time the world was flat.
No I'm not kidding.
It was really flat.
For all intents and purposes
it was very flat
because every mother,
and every father,
and every teacher
taught every child,
that was ever born that
the world is flat.

When good 'ole Christopher was born they tried to stuff it into his head that the world is flat. His parents and teachers weren't being mean. They were all doing the best they could. They wanted to teach things right and give him the truth and the facts. After all, they had also been born into "the world is flat" conversation. **We are all born in WAS.** We all end up with the interpretation systems and belief systems of **WAS**. And we'll stay in the belief conversation of **WAS** until we interpret life in a new way which will then create a belief system that the world may not be as flat as we once thought.

But I digress; let me get back to Christopher's story. I'm quite sure that when Christopher first argued that the world ain't flat he flunked geography.

Yep—I get it!

It isn't 1492 anymore so you may be smiling with superiority and thinking, "What an asinine example." That doesn't prove we are born into an already existing conversation/interpretation because nobody (well practically nobody) believes the world is flat now. Here's the question you should be asking yourself: What's my own personal "the world is flat" interpretation? What (both conscious and so ingrained that they are unconscious) belief systems drive my thoughts, feelings, choices, and actions?

> Facts = Content
> Interpretation = Context
> — toniraye

Many people live their life as if the story we have about any situation is *"The Truth."* In actuality, the facts are the content of whatever drama is happening in your life at the present time. You may not have power over the facts. However, you always have a great deal of power as to how you interpret those facts.

In the story, Pure Joy as a girl heard people talking in

the bathroom at school. It didn't matter if the other girls were talking about her or not. As soon as she decided they were laughing at her, that interpretation impacted her life for years to come. It's logical to draw the conclusion that regardless of what the girls in the restroom were talking about that incident became a triggering event for Pure Joy. Being rigorous in our in our thinking here we notice that the event isn't what caused Pure Joy's problems. This trigger event had no real power to have an effect on her life. It was her interpretation of the event that did the real damage and caused it to become a trigger.

She formed beliefs such as:

1. When I am open and I share I might end up embarrassed.
2. If I act too smart no one will like me.
3. Rather than be embarrassed or laughed at by others, it would be better to make fun of myself.
4. So what if people don't call me by my whole name, I should settle for less.
5. Bottom line = who I am authentically is not good enough.

As you think and consider real events from your own life is the real damage created by the event? Or is the real damage caused by your interpretation of the event?

The events	=	the content of our day to day life.
The interpretation	=	context of our life.

It will always and I mean always be
the context we create and come from;
the interpretations we bring forth from
the content facts that will trip us up,
and has the potential to cause us
the greatest harm.

For just one day, notice how many times you add interpretation to facts and then create beliefs and ensuing judgments that either empower you or disempower you. For example, a driver cuts you off on the highway. The fact is that someone put their car in front of yours. Your interpretation is your judgment and assessment of what happened. As soon as you think that stupid driver was rude, what are "they" thinking to give her a driver's license; you have created a conversation, an interpretation of the facts that creates a belief that:

(a) You are the victim of the other driver who has caused you to have a headache and
(b) You are the victim of whoever "they" the system is that issued the license.

Interpretation is your belief that how the other driver acts on the highway has anything to do with you. Do you really think the driver woke up this morning and said, "I can't wait to be rude to someone in traffic?" Your interpretation won't affect the other person's life but your day is tense because of how you judged the driver. The other driver may have problems but one thing I know for sure; his problems don't cause your problems. Your interpretation causes your problems.

Take a moment to re-interpret this situation in a way that is more powerful. See how the simple practice of powerful interpretation of events and situations might positively impact your mood, your day, your life.

My Feelings Come from An Interpretation

At the time of your birth you are whole and complete. Guess what? You were born into this world without your own personal interpretation, story, conversation, or view of "things." You feel whatever you feel and you don't judge those feelings as either right or wrong. They just are. A feeling is just a feeling – judging the feeling is creating an interpretation around the feeling. Observe a small child. One minute they are crying and sad. In the blink of an eye they have felt that feeling and they move on to joy and bliss. This is part of what creates life as an adventure for children. They feel it and then they experience and feel something brand new. A baby doesn't feel guilty because they messed in their pants. They cry a bit because that works to get clean pants then they move on to what's next in their day. Children can be our best teachers once we see them as valuable, instead of something we need to fix.

> A feeling is just a feeling – judging the feeling is creating an interpretation around the feeling.
> — toniraye

In the story, Pure Joy found uninhibited bliss in pushing

the elevator button, eating dinner at a new restaurant with her family, rolling in the grass playing with a puppy, and having tea parties with her imaginary friend, Destiny. Even being afraid of the escalator was something she could share.

However, as we grow, we learn to judge ourselves and others. Yes, it's a good idea to get potty trained and not mess in our pants. But what really disrupts our relationships and our ability to live life at 100% is our judgment that we have to hide every time we aren't perfect. That is when we begin to replace our authentic feelings with the idea that we are our feelings. We learn to shut down certain experiences. We generalize and make broad statements such as:

I Am afraid
I Am happy
I Am angry
I Am depressed
I Am excited
I Am strong
I Am disorganized

Be careful as these statements are absolutely not true! How we language ourselves begins to mold and change our life. As soon as we put something into words, we begin the process of labeling and framing our self to be those words. As we say it and think it over and over, we make it the truth of who we are. Then we set about proving ourselves right by being our label.

* You have feelings but you are not your feelings.
* You can have your feelings but your feelings are not you.
* You may have circumstances, but your circumstances don't have to have you because your circumstances are not who you are.

Learning was supposed to teach you not to touch a hot stove. Instead, some of us learned to be so afraid of the stove and the heat it produces that we no longer experience the joy of eating hot food. We have become afraid to turn on the stove and turn up the heat.

You can change the incorrect interpretation
of who you say you are.
You are not a fixed object.
You, my friend, are really on your way to Becoming,
moment to moment.

Try this. The next time you tell yourself, "I Am afraid," stop and reinvent your interpretation. Say it out loud or bring it to your conscious mind and think about it for a moment, "I am not afraid. I am __(your name)__. I am experiencing fear in this moment but a new moment will begin soon." As you practice, you will see a clear distinction between who you are versus what you feel. Below are a few examples of

> Mastering The Art Of Small Distinctions Will Change Your Life
> — toniraye

words we use to keep ourselves stuck in the Land Of Was:

I Am depressed versus I feel sort of flat today.

I Am excited versus I feel excited about my life today.

I Am stressed creates a lifetime of stress and is different from I feel stressed at the moment.

Being conscious of the principles surrounding life as an interpretation all the way to the core of who we are, means we make it all up!! Not what happened, but what you've done with it. If you are going to make up a story about "I Am," and you have a choice on which version to pick, Why not make the story an empowering one?

Now is the time for you to begin planning what you want and dream of on your own life's script. This is a great time to re-script your basic interpretations about what you decide to believe. After you finish reading the chapters on transformational principles, you will move on to a 30-day workbook which will support you in any new interpretations you want to flesh out.

I'm not suggesting we throw the baby out with the bath water. A lot of your interpretations work for you. How do I know? You wouldn't have read this far if you weren't already aware. This is just an oil change and a tune up to the already magnificent you.

> Keep the interpretations that work, ditch what doesn't. Decide what adventure is next.
> — toniraye

Chapter 2

I Believe, Therefore I Am

?? HOW DID I END UP IN WAS ??
Belief Systems - That's How!!

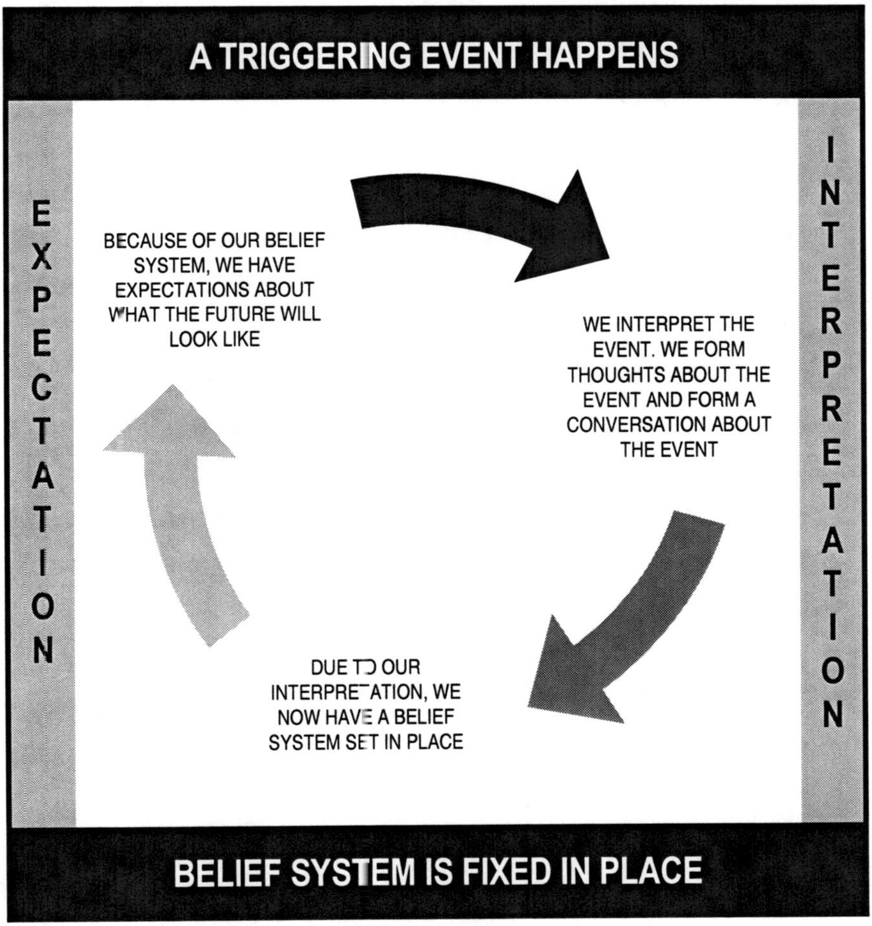

Charts are available for download at toniraye.com

As you view the belief system chart on the previous page and integrate our discussion in the previous chapter on interpretation we begin to see a relationship between these two separate but equal distinctions:

1) **Triggering event happens** — It could be something we judge as great or dreadful. Example: Your parents celebrating their 50-year wedding anniversary could be a trigger event in your life.

2) **The event triggers thought. The thought triggers your experience** — Your thoughts begin to generate and shade **"Your unique personal experience"** of things prior to, during, and after the event.
   Fact = There was a wedding celebration at the Hilton Hotel on Main Street. I mailed out the invitations. There were 31 adults, 13 children, and 6 grandchildren present.
   My experience of the facts = Everyone looks happy. My parents are delighted with the party. What a great family gathering.

3) **Feelings are generated** — My unique personal experience/perspective of the event creates a feeling inside my body (Happy, Excited, Sad, Angry, frightened, etc.)
   Feelings = I'm deliriously happy tonight

4) **Interpretation Happens** — Based on this feeling I now create an interpretation surrounding the facts of the event.

Interpretation = There are rewards when people make long term commitments to each other.

5) **Conclusions are drawn** — Depending on my interpretation I draw conclusions and make solid fixed decisions that might sound like:

Love is or is not ______________________

Commitment is or is not ______________________

Men Are ______________________

Women Are ______________________

Other People Are ______________________

The World Is or Is Not ______________________

People With Money Are ______________________

Fat People Are ______________________

Beautiful/Handsome People Are______________________

I Am ______________________

THEREFORE HE, SHE, THEY, WE, AND/OR IT
MUST OR MUST NOT
SHOULD OR SHOULD NOT
CAN OR CAN'T
WILL OR WON'T ETC.

6) **Beliefs are formed** — Based on the conclusions and decisions I made from my interpretations I fix in place an intricate set of beliefs to help me make some sense of life. The beliefs can be so called "good beliefs" or the so called "bad beliefs." I suggest that good and/or

bad doesn't apply here as the very nature of belief in this context locks us down and boxes us in. There isn't enough paper or print to list them all but our limiting beliefs will sound something like this:

To Be Loved I Must ______________________________

In Order To Love Others I Must ___________________

In Order To Trust Myself and Others I Must _________

In Order To Trust (Fred, Mary, My Husband Wife)
I Must ____

I Do Not Matter ___________________________________
(This is a more than/less than conversation)

I Matter A lot ____________________________________
(This is a more than/less than conversation)

I Have The Ability To Succeed If and/or When ______

I'm Smart Enough To _____________________________

I Am Worthy If and Only If ________________________

HERE IS THE BOTTOM LINE

BECAUSE OF MY PAST AND/OR PRESENT CIRCUMSTANCES

______________ **Is Possible For Me and/or Others**

______________ **Is Not Possible For Me and/or Others**

7) **Your Beliefs become an unconscious part of who you are** – In order to make sense of life and get through the daily tasks necessary, we aren't constantly pulling up the list of our beliefs and running a public check and balance to see where we stand on things. We wouldn't have time to breathe if we did that all day long. As the efficient machines we are, once we've decided on the "right way/wrong way" of things, we tell ourselves, "well then, that's all settled–no need to think on it anymore." We move all of these decisions about our beliefs to the unconscious part of our brain. We move it to unconscious automatic behavior mode and tell our EGO to keep it sorted out for us. The problem here is that my ego insists that:

I LOOK GOOD...
(I'm Superior Because of My Unique Set of Beliefs)

BE RIGHT
(About My Unique Set of Beliefs)

MAINTAIN RIGID CONTROL
(so my beliefs remain intact)
(so I can stay superior and continue to be right)

8) **Self-fulfilling Prophecy follows** — Once our beliefs are fixed in place, the ego has an expectation that we be right about the belief. When you think about it that makes perfect sense. If I believe 2 + 2 = 4 why would I be looking for or expecting 2 + 2 = 142 to show up in my universe. I begin to drift through my life making choices and doing the things that did and didn't work from yesterday. Wow. You're stuck in the Land of WAS with that babe! Drifting through our life repeating over and over again like a rat in a maze. Using the same outdated patterns of belief, creating yesterday's circumstances over and over yet wondering why history constantly repeats itself. We work hard and often get great results but may not end up enjoying the journey to the results we get.

WE SHUT DOWN DISCOVERY AND POSSIBILITY BECAUSE THERE IS NO NEED TO DISCOVER WHAT I ALREADY KNOW!

For the purpose of being a contribution and to help make the point, I am going to use an example of something I know about—some of the interpretations and believe systems that I have used in my past. Beliefs which didn't give me results I wanted, but did give me results consistent with what I believed.

1st STEP — TRIGGER EVENTS + ALREADY EXISTING BORN INTO CONVERSATION:

1. As a child my parents divorced.
   (Trigger event)
2. I heard someone say my dad was a cheater.
   (Trigger event)
3. We moved to another city away from my dad.
   (Trigger event)
4. My Dad drove 150 miles every weekend to see me.
   (Trigger event)
5. One of the cultural conversations around me was that Italian women are fat once they have babies. I don't remember how I knew, but this wasn't a positive thing.

2nd STEP — I GAVE MUCH THOUGHT AND ATTENTION TO THE "GORY DETAILS" (story about the divorce) AND TRIED TO MAKE SENSE OF WHAT WAS HAPPENING TO ME BECAUSE OF THE STORY HAPPENING ALL AROUND ME:

My Thoughts as a child were in turmoil during this period and too numerous to write about; however, some of the main interpretations I formed were about men and what it takes for a woman to be loved. Most beliefs formed out of this childhood trigger event don't work for lasting committed relationships.

3rd STEP — I FORMED NOT JUST ONE BUT MANY BELIEF SYSTEMS OUT OF MY INTERPRETATION OF ALL THAT WAS HAPPENING:

1. Handsome men cheat.
2. If I am good enough even though they cheat they'll pay attention to me.
3. I need the attention to be ok because I can't take care of myself.
4. I MUST HAVE LOVE OR I'LL BE FRIGHTENED, BROKE, AND ALONE.
5. I will only be loved when I perform perfectly and behave perfectly.
6. The cheating will be after I get fat.
7. No handsome guy wants a fat Italian girl.
8. If he does want me he must be hiding something or something is definitely wrong with him because why would he pick me when I'm not perfect and I'm going be fat? No sense to fight it—so I'd better try to hide it.
9. Even if people think I'm pretty it's just because I'm fooling them because I'll always be fat. (belief that follows that = I'm phoney)
10. If I cut the guy first it won't hurt so much so I'd better have an exit strategy for tough times to come.

All these intersecting belief systems constitute what might be called a double bind. It isn't just one belief system producing my choices. It's a whole great big bunch of "stuff" running my choices. If I don't even realize these belief systems are there, I have no power to interpret in a new way and create a more powerful set of belief systems. I learned 2 + 2 = 4 but no one taught me about the danger of not paying attention to limiting belief systems. Therefore, the 4th step was automatic. The double bind here is that I need a man to be ok but all men are cheaters so what to do?

Life needs to be consistent so I made choices consistent with what I already believed. I needed a man. I only dated handsome guys. The kinds of guys I picked liked slim girls. When it was time to find a guy I would diet like crazy and act like a confident thin girl. Guess what happened: they cheated. I ate. I got fat. There you go. All handsome guys cheat and all Italian girls get fat after middle age sets in.

While I don't know your particular brand of limiting beliefs, there are a core group of basics that almost all of us have buried in our head somewhere:

1. I will die and therefore, I am disposable.
2. I don't matter.
3. I'm not enough.
4. I need to love myself before I can love anyone else.

In addition to the above core, we begin creating a special group of beliefs for our own self. By the way, we all have beliefs that DO work for us. Examples: I am smart and capable, people support me, failure is part of the process to succeed, etc. We are addressing the limiting ones that get in the way of what we really want. Notice what some of your own LIMITING beliefs are, how they stop you. Examples: I can't trust men/women, the world isn't safe, I am shy and others are more capable than me, etc. If I believe a person can't have a successful career AND a successful relationship, then one of them is doomed to fail.

Try this experiment for 30 days and notice the change in your results and satisfaction. Regardless of the truth and regardless of any situation going on in your life, **believe and act** on the assumption that:

1. Everybody in your life and the universe in general has your best interest at heart.
2. Believe that everyone is doing the best they know how to do or else they would already be doing things differently.

Your children,
the neighbor across the street,
the person you're in a lawsuit with,
the checkout person in the grocery story,
your boss,
the congress of the United States,
EVERYBODY

P.S. This doesn't mean walk down a dark street at night or leave your doors unlocked. H E L L O – But take the experiment past your comfort zone as if "everybody in the world has my best interest at heart" is a possibility.

Chapter 3

I Am, Therefore I Am

I AM NO THING

The Distinction of the Occurring World versus Fixed World

Why is it most of us learn 90% of everything we're going to learn in the first 7 years of life? Why as we grow older do we slow down our learning? When did discovery stop being the point? Discovery and possibility begin to shut down at the age when you decide about what is right and what is wrong. When you develop a fixed picture of how things are, how things look, how "IT" should be. As you begin to know the truth, the capital "TRUTH."

Our ability to form judgments and to interpret is the weapon (defense mechanism) we use to limit our discovery; to limit the possibilities out of which we choose. There's no possibility for anything new out of what I already know or out of the truth as seen by my peers, my teachers, my culture, my environment, or my parents. We subtly gather information about all the "fixed in place rules" in the Land of Was at an early age. Then we use this kind of knowledge to start defending how we're right about what we already know. Once I already "know" there is no point in going for the gold, I start living my life not to lose instead of to win. You see, in order to really discover, in order to win the game of life big, you're going to have to be wrong about the truth of your belief that you don't matter. Even those of us with a belief that I'm pretty darn good; pretty darn high up the ladder of success is an arrogant belief called, "I know it all" therefore, I'm more, I'm better, I'm different. If my conversation comes from this more-better-different place I'm still judging and assessing how much I matter. Judging and assessing makes some things possible but shuts down other possibilities. As soon as I judge I am deciding right or wrong. Any nailed-in-place belief means you ain't goin' nowhere. You are already at the end of a dead end road.

Living in the Land of Was, we wake up every day believing that life controls us. Things, circumstances and people control us. With this interpretation, we believe that today looks just like yesterday. I already know what yesterday looked like – therefore, I surely know what today will be like. Nothing special is required of me because I don't matter, and if my results are going to look like yesterday's results then I can think and stay the same as I was yesterday in WAS. And the flip side of the same coin, where I'm more-better-different than you, keeps me fixed in my arrogant mediocrity because if I'm better already that's quite good enough. There is no need to change because I'm doing ok in the Land of Was just as I am. Yesterday, today, and tomorrow that's just the way things are in the Land of Was.

No wonder life gets boring. The alarm goes off today at the same time it did yesterday, and I go to the same job today that I went to yesterday, and I drive the same way to work today that I took to get to work yesterday.

But today does not have to look like yesterday. "Today is

just like yesterday" is a trap we don't have to fall into. Today is not yesterday.

Today is a brand new day. Just because you were
sad
happy
depressed
scattered and unfocused,
guilty of not being the best You,
better than someone else
YESTERDAY
doesn't have anything to do with who you decide to be today. Today is a whole, new Becoming day. I'm not suggesting that if you were broke and can't pay the electric bill you should put your head in the sand and see this fact as different from yesterday. But you do have the power to change things today.

The good news is that at the exact minute you realize you have fallen into the trap of drifting through your life, you are at choice. Here's a news flash. It's ok to leave second base and have a home run. But you will never leave second base if you see what you have already accomplished as the biggest home run possible. From that position you don't even notice that you're still sitting on second base with more innings left to play. And from that position someone is going to knock you off second base as they are running for home.

Moment to moment in the twinkling of an eye
I have the ability to choose a new way of being.

As I choose a new occurring me
My life will certainly change as well.
Being-Doing-Having
is an orderly process which is part
of the constantly changing evolving occurring you.
Who I am Being—Creates The Choices I See
As Possible For Me
Which Creates—The Things I Do
What I Do Creates What I Have

There are people out there who have viewed the law of attraction as a fixed thing. Their belief system around "The Law of Attraction" sounds like, I don't need to change anything, I don't need to do anything. I'll just sit here and think about prosperity and sha-zamm one day I'll be rich. I suggest that in order for "The Law of Attraction" to work in your life you must first lay down your mistaken beliefs about who you are in the world for yourself and others. As you lay down these beliefs your "beingness" will naturally change.

If my belief is that the world is fixed and I don't matter I might wake up a grump butt everyday and no law of attraction in the world will cause people to want to be in a business relationship with me. Unless I get lucky and win the lotto I will stay broke and grumpy. If I am "superman" (or superwoman) and wake up superior to "them" (superior to those other people outside of me) I probably shouldn't expect the law of attraction to bring me a fabulous relationship. The perfect fab person could be right there and

I wouldn't recognize it because I'm too busy being my fixed way of being that doesn't pick fab people to hang around with. After all, if I am around fab people I might not get to be superior anymore because they'd be more fab than me.

As I begin to view the world as a wondrous occurring adventure I might wake up feeling like a grump butt and in a flash remember who I am: not a grump butt at all...I am a contributing, powerful, gift to the business world. And from that possible view of myself I will attract all the good things life has to offer. Or I wake up and notice I'm being judgmental. Then I choose to appreciate people in my life, and I notice my relationships start to change.

It won't work to sit on the couch and beat my overweight self up. Neither will it do any good to practice strict will power and go on a diet, then gain it all back when I stop. However, as the possibility of who I am flourishes and grows my being will attract—the correct doing—to cause the exact results I want.

You are Becoming, moment to moment, a wondrous, cosmic being. You may not have all that is possible for you landed perfectly yet. However, once the idea slams into your conscious mind that you are not a fixed thing and neither is the rest of the world, new possible futures open up.

With distinctions such as, life as an interpretation, belief systems, and the idea of an occurring world in place we can connect the "law of attraction" to what we've already learned. Any time something is created it is created twice; first in the inventor (creator's) mind. There it germinates and the idea of what we want shifts and changes and solidifies to become thoughts of what we really want and how we want this new possible idea to actually manifest in the real world. We might think of this step as where the context of what we want to create starts. The second part is to go out there and actually do the things necessary for your creative results to show up in the material world.

Escape From Was is a modern day fable with three basic parts:

Stage I: Pure Joy and Will are born whole and complete as possibility.
They are born into an occurring becoming space of what's possible.
But there is an already waiting existing conversation of "not possible" waiting for them.

Stage II: A loss of innocence happens in childhood.
They begin to judge and label themselves and others.
As they take on fixed belief systems a joyful view of life's possibilities is no longer consistent with what they "already know" to be true.

They have moved to the fixed Land of Was!

Stage III: The Discovery - The Rebirth (The uncovering and revealing) of the Authentic Self.

During the ATM machine chapter, P.J. is bored with everything and she sees her life, her marriage, her relationships as hopeless. Life has become so fixed that it is something to survive - something she has to do. She doesn't choose to—she has to: **YOU FILL IN THE BLANK.** Will zones out every night in front of the television. She zones out daily by messing around playing computer games and/or shopping.

She rushes from here to there but is missing something. It has been many years since she remembered she was born to be Pure Joy. She has almost completely forgotten that life used to be about tea parties. Will has forgotten that he was born to be Free Adventurous Will. Even though we have forgotten, we can have a rebirth and create and renew the vision for our life. There persists in the deepest fundamental levels of our true self vague feelings that life could be more. He could be more, she could be more, you could be more, the world could rise to a new standard of being.

In our story, Pure Joy definitely yearns for the connection and sense of sharing she had with other people as a child. Dear reader, no matter how great your life is right now, isn't it true that you yearn to return to your pure authentic self? Anyone that's ever stood in a crowd of people yet felt alone knows that as part of the human race we want to connect and belong. That is how P.J.'s life is in our story. From the outside looking in she has the perfect life, but she has lost her sense of destiny.

One day she woke up. We don't know why, but she really woke up and she remembered who she was. In life it isn't one thing that causes us to lay down the adventure of life and it usually isn't a lightning strike from heaven that wakes us up. This one thing is true for me however, when I am in the question of possibility; when I remain open to answers that are seemingly hidden and yet right there in front of me, an inner knowingness occurs and blossoms into whatever it is I need or desire in that space of time.

When you are in a space of commitment and inquiry, you will always attract the resources needed to create whatever you have declared is important to you. And that is one of many reasons that life is an awesome powerful journey.

In the exact moment that P.J. remembered she was born to be Pure Joy her life was irrevocably changed forever. The following passage from our story is a vital key to a future worth creating:

Dear ATM Machine—
You may know my bank account number,
And how many zeros I have in my account balance.
But!!! *You don't know me!*
Let me repeat!!! You don't know me!
I am not hard wired—because I'm not a machine.
I am an occurring, evolving
Pure Joy person
(Or, at least, I used to be)
And
I am now ready to be Pure Joy again.

I name myself, and how I name myself is how others define me.

The self you are is merely interpretation rather than a thing. **As you remove all the layers of interpretation away that we think we are, there is nothing left except flesh and bones and possibility.**

In an occurring (becoming) world
creation is in process at all times.

I am nothing
I am no thing.
I am no fixed thing.
Out of this "no thing" place
I am free to create anything
that I say matters.

Chapter 4

I Experience, Therefore I Am

GENERATING MY EXPERIENCE OF LIFE

As you read through the following statements notice the juxtaposition, relatedness, and separation between the various parts. Jot down a few notes about ideas and thoughts that come to you as you examine this passage:

You always have a way of being emanating in the foreground that affects how others relate to you due to their experience of you.

You always have a Context you come from operating in the background.

There is doing and having going on in the foreground.

You are the driver of your life. The Context you come from causes you to drive in a particular direction.

Content is the tool/vehicle that the driver uses to get to the destination.

There is the Master at the helm plotting the course and setting sail.

There is Content...
The size, color, age and
gender of the ship.
But That Isn't
What Steers The Ship
Into the Ocean

There is the experience of
the journey
And
There is the experience of
the destination.

There is the experience
And
There is the memory of
the experience.

In our culture we tend to think of

Our car,
My diamond bracelet
Her house,
His bank account and credit score,
The career,
Tall or short,
Thin - curvy
Doctor - Lawyer - Indian Chief
Recognition for my past work
Recognition as the man of
the year
Recognition as mom
of the year

ALL THE OUTWARD MANIFESTATIONS,
To be the stuff that dreams are made of
To be the "one true thing" that will cause eternal happiness.

You read the statements above and know this isn't true but in the Land of Was the marketing pulls us back to this "good stuff." How other people view us creates angst. All of this content and all the angst over the content generate an atmosphere where we must:

Prove ourselves to others You no longer have results
You are your results
You Are Your Stuff.

This is all just peachy if it is producing the experience of life you are aiming for. However, if you often produce outstanding results, yet are seldom satisfied with the outcomes you end up with it means that something from the context that you are coming from is off balance. In our story Will had lots of stuff, a great wife, great kids, a good job, and a new car. He still wasn't happy and his golf clubs were rusty in the garage. What's up with that? Do you believe we are supposed to work hard, do the right thing, and still be miserable? Maybe we don't have time to enjoy our results because we are constantly busy:

Comparing Ourselves To Our Past
Comparing Ourselves To Others
Comparing Ourselves To What Should Be

Which Catapults Us Into A Context Called
MORE-BETTER-DIFFERENT.

Living the Context of MORE-BETTER-DIFFERENT
Looks Like-Sounds Like-Feels Something Like:

As soon as I have a more...
perfect body and perfectly enhanced/augmented breasts
As soon as I have more...
chiseled manly muscles and 6 pack abs
As soon as I have more...
Money because I have More Education
As soon as I have the right...
husband/wife/partner (a more perfect life mate)
As soon as my kids behave the right way
(MORE well behaved—MORE disciplined Kids)
As soon as there is more peace in the world

As soon as there is more ----- FILL IN THE BLANK -----
than there is right now

BOTTOM LINE = AS SOON AS I HAVE MORE
THEN (AND ONLY THEN) THINGS WILL BE BETTER
THEN (AND ONLY THEN) I WILL BE, AND MY LIFE WILL BE,
(IN THE NEAR OR DISTANT FUTURE
BUT NOT IN THE PRESENT)
MUCH BETTER AND DIFFERENT THAN IT IS RIGHT NOW!

The context of living from the More-Better-Different space involves a belief system

Which Assumes ***Content precedes Context***.

> Here's a clue about life—
> Everything we learn in the Land of Was is backwards to how the natural flow of life works.
> -toniraye

It is silly to think of the car (the content) as anything that can make us happy. The car is the tool the driver uses to get where we want to go. But driving the car safely and being able to steer the car in directions I say matter is where the real adventure happens. *The adventure brings the joy.* The context brings the joy. The content is the tool that helps us take the journey at the pace we want. What's around the next bend is adventure. The real joy happens from being on the journey. Once we reach the destination the journey is over (that adventure is complete). **What isn't—is more important than what is.** The next breath is always more important than the last breath. Once the journey is over we are only thinking about and remembering the journey we once had. Remembering is content—We are remembering the content of the journey we already had. Remembering the JOY is great but it isn't as great as experiencing the JOY for real. Having content—Having a car isn't the journey it is a tool that helps me on my journey.

Therefore, don't mistake things for the real adventure.

The real joy, the real journey, is feeling the wind blow across my face as I drive toward the ocean. I can sense the ocean breeze, I feel the moisture in the air, and the sun kisses my checks. There is such joy in driving the vehicle from the darkness of the midnight hour to the awakening of the sun rising over the tip of the mountain pass.

I am not suggesting that the content of life isn't part of the fun of life. The sun kissing my face and the smell of the ocean breeze is content that certainly allowed me to experience the journey in a rich full way. And I like the smell of a new car as much as the next girl. I am suggesting however, that the context we come from allows us to experience ourselves, the relationships surrounding us, and the things we have quite differently.

An alternative context which will produce an entirely different experience of life's journey is the **"choose to" versus "have to"** model. You could drop the driving influences bombarding you externally and choose what you want from your internal drive. The trick is to stay aware of where the drive is coming from. If it is coming from I have to go to work and support my family you will get in the car and pull yourself through the day. If you shift internally to choosing to be a contribution to your family and the satisfaction it gives when you contribute

> Are you thinking this is way too simplistic?

to others, your experience of working will change. You are choosing contribution. Working is the vehicle to allow your choice of contribution to happen. With this perspective of life you still get all the "stuff" and outcomes in life you want. In fact, you have an unlimited smorgasbord to choose from. You don't need anyone's permission or authority to allow you to "choose to." You don't do anything because he/she/they/it makes you "DO IT." You are at choice based on your own unique context. You make a conscious choice about your way of being to the exact same circumstance or event—like your daily job or family. Ask yourself what way of being will produce what I want? You look at an abundance of menu choices and pick what you want. Suggested healthy way of being menu choices might be living as my word, living from my commitments, living in contribution, life is an adventure, I have something important to give to the world, I am worthy of receiving, I choose to be authentic, vulnerable, open, have time for myself to renew, am powerful in deciding what matters to my life, etc. These menu choices are the special of the day but I don't presume to know what your favorite meal on the menu should be.

> What if it is just that simple?

> Have To Falls By The Wayside Because
> Choose To Takes Its Place.
> -toniraye

Once you have decided on your way of being choice you are ready to pick the second course. This course contains some vegetables. Let's call this "It's time to eat my veggies part of the meal." What actions and doing needs to happen as a natural outgrowth from the context I already decided on?

Then the dessert arrives. You don't order the dessert at this point. You already put in the dessert order when you made your way of being choice earlier.

Prior to preparing a meal, you look at the pictures in the recipe book and decide what meal you want to cook for dinner or you decide to go out for dinner.
YOU HAVE LOTS OF CHOICES

At a restaurant, you read about the items on the menu before choosing what to order.

There is the experience of the texture, smell and taste as you eat the meal.

We don't get nourishment by eating the cardboard menu.

The nourishment comes from choosing what you want to eat and eating.

In our past, some of us have mistaken the menu for the meal in life.

THAT DOESN'T WORK SO GOOD.
LET'S NOT CHOOSE TO DO THAT AGAIN

Your Belief In Your Ability To Create Is Part Of Your Context

We Don't Create By Magic. There is a logical flow to the way we generate and produce results. Being aware of the process will support you in consciously producing what you decide you want.

Thoughts	Create	Feelings
Feelings	Create	Attitude
Attitude	Creates	My Experience and Choices
Choices	Create	My Actions
Vision/Dreams	Create	Actions
Actions	Create	Results

Participation Creates Value

Value and Consequence Creates Urgency

Risking Creates Energy and Excitement

Desire Creates Intention
Intention Creates Opportunity

Awareness Creates Recognition
Recognition and Character Creates Action
Action Creates Results

Chapter 5

I Am, Therefore I Matter

VICTIM VERSUS RESPONSIBLE
I AM 100% RESPONSIBLE, 100% OF THE TIME FOR THE RESULTS IN MY LIFE

Here is what I know for sure about the victim responsible conversation in life. After 20 years of learning and commitment to my own personal growth I still love my story—my History (history = his story and her hysteria). I often love the drama and sadness of "I'm helpless" and alone more than my commitment to my ideals and world vision. I used to spend maybe 90% of my life in a victim conversation. Though I still go back there to visit from time to time, I am proficient at catching myself in the act of victimhood. As soon as I notice I'm visiting there, I am at choice about whether I stay or get out of the Land of Was. If I decide to stay awhile, I run my victim story and then I'm tired of it. I peek out from under the blanket of WAS, put on sunglasses (so I won't be blinded by the light of possibility), and take responsibility for my commitments, choices, and actions. On the occasions that I take action and allow my being to come from my stand to live in a world that works—WOW. During those moments I am energized and accomplish more than I would have dreamed was possible.

> If everyone committed to personal growth could stay conscious of the being 100% responsible piece—only 10% of the time—we would experience world peace.

So what is the difference between being a victim and being responsible? Worldwide, I have found responsibility to be the most misunderstood distinction there is. When growing up, most of us had responsibility linked with guilt and blame. "I screwed up—I feel bad and I'm responsible." Or we had it linked with obligation, a have-to, the weight of the world on our shoulders. I'm responsible and I HAVE TO take care of everything. Neither of these have anything to do with responsibility. In fact, they are part of the victim conversation.

Responsibility is the ability to respond. I am in ownership of my thoughts, my feelings, my actions, ALL the results around me. They are not being done to me. They are mine. That does not mean I like the results I have (example: things are a mess with the family and my brother's actions have left my Mom upset) but if I own them I have the ability to respond and I can take action to affect the outcome. It is easy to be responsible when everything is going great. The point of power and freedom is to choose to be responsible when things are in turmoil and don't seem to be fair.

At their birth, both Pure Joy and Free Will had an authentic natural way of being that was whole and complete. They weren't broken. They didn't need to be fixed in a certain "Was" way. During the naming ceremony their parents cradled them gently, raised them aloft, and saw them as a gift to the universe. Pure Joy was naturally an open, creative, lovable, sharing bundle of "Pure Joy" sort of girl. Will was this rambunctious, "I am the master of my own ship" kind of "Free Will" guy.

As we move through the story of our life however, a change occurs; a transformation happens. Past experience teaches us, “Don’t be so open, better be careful because someone wants your place on the ladder.” Do we become cynical? Maybe. At the least I’d say we lose or simply misplace some of the essence of who we were born to be. As a parent, I might say it is my job to teach my children not to get hurt and to fit into the Land of Was. As a parent, it was my intention to have my son transform into a productive conforming member of the culture of WAS. If any of us knew how to do better we would already be doing better. But I only knew how to teach the way I’d been taught and my parents taught me what they learned in WAS, as well.

It isn’t our intention consciously to transform into adults
that aren’t authentic.
But that is often what happens in the Land of Was.

As we compare ourselves to others,
jealousy and envy surely follow.

As we compare ourselves to our past,
guilt and fear that we aren’t enough becomes the norm.

As we compare ourselves to how it should be,
we create a conversation that life isn’t fair.

With all of the above, we go straight to victimhood. Why

do we keep going to our victim story when just thinking and telling the story makes us miserable? Absolutely everything has both a reward and a price. I buy a new dress and it has a price tag, but I look so cute in my new outfit! So do I want to pay the price and take home the reward or not?

There is a cost and a reward for being responsible. There is a price and a reward when we live in our victim story. We just haven't been taught to notice the price/reward ratio consciously, so our ego makes the decisions for us. I don't know about you but I don't want my ego to make my decisions for me. Here's an example of a single event but with two different interpretations from my own victim versus responsible story book.

Story #1:

I was married to a guy for twenty-five years. I gave him the best years of my life and stuck by him through thick and thin. Then you know what he did? He walked out on me on Christmas Day, that's exactly what he did. He left me broke and in despair with my life falling down around me because he wanted a size 4 younger woman. And besides all that, I was no longer young, thin, and attractive enough to get a new guy. I was so hurt and emotionally distraught that I couldn't look for a job or take care of myself. Once he came over to get some clothes he had left behind and I was curled up in a little ball in the closet sobbing. That's how terrible it was for me. In retrospect, I'm better off without the jerk and should have set him out with the trash years ago. If you are a reasonably intelligent person reading this right now you can see that I was definitely a victim of him. But don't you worry about me because no man will ever get the chance to treat me that way again. Most all men are cheaters; every smart woman knows that.

Here is a list of the rewards we get in being the victim:

1. I get to be right that it's not my fault.
2. I get to be right that there was nothing I could do about the situation.
3. I get to be superior about the fault and blame of others.
4. I don't have to risk anything to change the situation or the future.
5. I get pity, sympathy, and a lot of attention (people worry about me).
6. Someone else is bad but I'm righteous and good.
7. AND HERE IS MY PERSONAL FAVORITE

   As long as I was emotionally distraught he felt so guilty. I got to manipulate the situation to my best advantage and view of myself.

HERE IS A LIST OF THE PRICES WE PAY BY STAYING THE VICTIM:

1. Nothing changes; I'll repeat the pattern again to get the above rewards.
2. I never get what I really want.
3. I don't feel good about myself.
4. The cycle continues—I shut down my ability to think—I already know the future.
5. I experience resignation and low energy.

6. I don't get to experience the power and freedom of choosing to have things be awesome.
7. I don't get to give or receive because I'm inward focused.
8. My health suffers—I'm tense and filled with anxiety.

Story #II:

I was married to a really wonderful man for twenty five years. In fact, he's still a wonderful man. We owned a telephone business and worked hard for years to make that business a success. I remember once my husband told me how much he hated the phone business. He said, "We don't own the business, the business owns us." He wanted to build a different kind of business. He was an entrepreneur with an exuberant spirit. But I didn't want to start something new. It would have been so much work to do that. In addition, I was sure that if we didn't keep all our eggs in one basket that the eggs would get broken. In fact, I told him exactly that. I said, "You know I want to support you but now isn't a good time. Maybe we can do that later but for now you need to concentrate on what we already have." I couldn't see any reason to diversify. After all, we were comfortable. Why move off of second base? I just wanted us to maintain the status quo.

A few years later on Christmas Day he came to me and said, "From Vietnam to now, no matter what I do it's not good enough. I can't even take out the trash right." When he said that, I didn't say anything out loud, but I was thinking,

"If you'd just twist the bag twice before you put it in the trash barrel you could do it right." There was no one that could do anything as perfect as I could. I was "so perfect" that it didn't leave any room for him to be of value to me.

In retrospect, I don't know why he tried as long as he did. I was afraid that if I made any mistakes we wouldn't have enough money or security. We wouldn't have enough, period. Instead of sharing my fears I shut the fear beneath hard work. There was no way I would have risked talking about such "negative feelings." I put up a wall of superiority, that's for sure.

During twenty five years of marriage, I can't remember any fights. We didn't need to fight; we just did things my way, because my way was always the right way. So, I was really surprised at his next words. He said, "Sweetheart, I know you may not believe this right now but I really love you and there is something in you that I believe can be great. I just don't have the energy to keep trying. I'm stepping off the merry-go-round." He said, "I'm holding you back so I'm leaving."

I know it seems bad that he left on Christmas Day, but I can promise you that he had been trying to tell me that things weren't working for several years before he left. I just didn't hear him until after he was gone. I learned so much about myself during this experience. One of my biggest areas of learning was about how I showed up for other people. His courage to tell me the truth and take responsibility for his happiness helped me learn how to be responsible for mine.

A LIST OF THE PRICES WE PAY IF WE CHOOSE TO BE RESPONSIBLE:

1. There are no excuses; no one is to blame.
2. I have to give up all beliefs that I don't matter.
3. I don't get to sit around passively and play it safe.

A LIST OF THE REWARDS WE GAIN WHEN WE CHOOSE TO BE RESPONSIBLE:

1. I get to decide what's important to me and take action on it.
2. I'm in ownership of what's occurring, so I can change it.
3. I get to experience freedom and power.
4. I have the chance to create the results I really want.
5. Life isn't boring.

Both stories contain the facts, so which one is true?

Having a life worth living isn't always about "the truth". It is all about perspective and how I interpret the facts. I can take responsibility for my part in the drama, learn from it, and move toward my destiny. I can beat myself up because of my part in the drama (thereby staying stuck in "I'm not worthy of happiness") for years. I can blame someone else and have an excuse for mediocrity. The choice is all mine.

ARMED WITH KNOWLEDGE OF
THE PRICES AND REWARDS IN CHOOSING TO BE RESPONSIBLE

In Any Given Moment I Can—You Can Make A Decision
To Drop The Mantle Of Victim
And
Adopt the role of Being Responsible
You aren't deciding who's right, who's wrong
Moment to Moment Your Decision Is About
What Works, What Doesn't, What's next.
Think About It—Does being closed off, shut down,
And living from a place of I have to
Bring harmony and vitality to relationships?
If your answer is NO—AND
You Have A Commitment To Bring Harmony
and Vitality To Relationships
What Are You Going To Do?

> There are options - There are choices here
> FOR GOSH SAKES TAKE A STEP BACK FROM EMOTION AND GET CONSCIOUS OF YOUR CHOICES

1. Complain that your kids aren't in a harmonious mood today then blame them because your commitment didn't happen?
2. File for Divorce.
3. Never talk to your parents again because they "messed" you up.
4. Complain that others don't "get it"—I'm not sure what "IT" is... But for sure they just don't "GET IT."
5. Stay miserable and pretend you're ok with the way things are.
6. Tell yourself that "other people" should know you care

about them after all, you show them with all your hard work.

7. Bury your head in the sand believing that you're a special case Therefore, life should be different for you.
8. Go to revenge – After all if they hurt my feelings, they're gonna' pay dearly because I don't get mad I just get even!

You aren't God, so one of the picks from your smorgasbord of life isn't to fix and change the people you are in relationship with.

You just don't have that kind of power. So don't go righteous here about how evolved you are and how "they" need for you to fix 'em.

BUT YOU DO HAVE ANOTHER POWERFUL — RESPONSIBLE CHOICE AVAILABLE!

At any given time,
On any given day,
At any given moment!

You can create a new interpretation and belief system about life.

That belief system might sound something like...
I and only I have the power to transform my life and the relationships in my life
I don't need anyone's permission
I don't need anyone's authority
I declare — I decide

To be contributing and to receive

To be authentic
To be happy

To have my life and my relationships work

To trust myself to "BE" Who I need to "BE"

I can surrender to a belief that it doesn't need to look a certain fixed way

I have a choice to believe that everybody gets to win

You, my friend, have the ability to transform yourself
You have power over your interpretation
and belief about yourself
And your capacity to accomplish
What you are truly committed to.

One possible choice is for you is to adopt a belief called,
"I am 100% Responsible, 100% of the time
For the relationships and results in my life."
A Belief Called
Moment by Moment: I Have the Ability
To Forfeit the Person Who Lives In Was
In Order To Become – The Person I Declare I AM.
Once I declare it, I have the power
To keep my word to myself
And live my declaration.

Chapter 6

I'm In The Game, Therefore I Am

LET THE GAME BEGIN

All the world's a stage,
And all the men and women merely players;
They have their exits and their entrances,
And one man in his time plays many parts.

—William Shakespeare

Let's pretend that on this world stage we are playing one gigantic game and it's the Super Bowl of all games ever invented. In addition (just to spice the game up a bit), we don't know how many minutes we have left to play in the game and there are no time outs. But we do know that at the end of this game we are either going into permanent retirement or we will be recruited to play in the all star games, which are held on a different planet entirely. I heard gossip that the All Star game is being held somewhere in outer space but I don't know the exact longitude or latitude. So don't be worried about that right now. Concentrate on playing this game to the best of your ability.

You never have to sit out on the bench while the "A" string plays. In this game, we're all the "A" string. If you decide to sit on the bench for awhile that's fine, jump back in when you're ready.

There are three major ways to play in the game: as the observer, the participant, or as the creator of the game. None of these roles are good or bad. However, some things are available to you and some things not available, depending on which position you're playing at any given time. There is a cost and a benefit to the way you decide to play, so some strategy would be useful. I suggest you take a class and get a coach to support your play, but that's entirely up to you.

One of the useful strategies to know is that we never pick just one way to play and stay there forever and ever. You will slide in and out from one position to the next. The more you jump in and play, the better you'll get at recognizing where you are on the field and what plays you're up to. If you notice that how you play isn't helping you or other teammates to win, you always have a moment by moment choice to play a different way.

It seems to me that this game is better than any of the video games out there because no matter how many times you make a mistake or jump out of bounds you will not be forced to quit the game. Of course, there are logical and natural consequences in how you decide to play. As an example, sometimes people on drugs think they are playing safely when they're not. Be careful about that because you and your family could get hurt. There is no punisher on the field but those kinds of things cause the natural and/or logical consequences I already mentioned.

One last thing of note: there are no opposing teams. Every human being (and I say dogs as well) are on your team. The object of the game is to accumulate the maximum number of positive points. Let me be really clear on this rule!!! The object of the game is for every single person on the planet to accumulate the maximum number of positive points.

It's either win—win or everybody loses!

The Observer Role

In This Role I Am Watching The Game. My Key Function Is Reporting, Describing, Judging, And Assessing Myself And The Other Players On The Field.

I have a great seat often sitting at home with the remote control in my hand and availability of instant replay.

I'm not suited up for the game nor on the field playing so I don't usually get my hands dirty or break a nail.

I don't get hurt!
How could I get hurt...
I'M NOT ACTUALLY PLAYING...
H E L L O !!!

I do need to be careful that I don't get too close to the field of play. Since I don't practice, I don't have strong bones and muscles.

The Observer Role

I NEVER LOSE
BECAUSE I'M NOT PLAYING
H E L L O !!!

I may have the illusion that I'm In Control.

I get to look good and be right in my judgment of how others are playing.

I might have $ or fame but my song might be, *"Is That All There Is."*

I avoid risk at all cost. My fear is buried and I may not realize how I'm playing.

I may feel sort of flat lined and depressed. I'm sometimes bored.

I am usually Passive or Passive Aggressive.

I NEVER WIN
BECAUSE I'M NOT PLAYING
H E L L O !!!

THE BELIEF HERE IS THAT
THERE IS NO WAY TO WIN!
WORLD PEACE ISN'T POSSIBLE!

LOSE — LOSE

The Participant Role

I'm On The Field Suited Up
For The Game
But Someone Else Is Calling In The Plays.

**I Will Play As Long
As You Tell Me Exactly
What To Do**

I Am Taking Action
But When I Make Mistakes
I Am Afraid Of Failure
Or Embarrassment

**I Want To See
The Results And A
Winning Score Quickly
I Get Discouraged
and Quit Easily**

My Results Are Erratic
Sometimes I Make
Great Plays
Sometimes I Set Out
For A Few Turns

My Results
At Any Given Moment
Depend On How I Feel Today

The Participant Role

I Live In The Context Of
Fault-Blame-Credit
I Strongly Believe In
Good Luck and Bad Luck

When I Win—
Good Luck Gets The Credit
When I Lose—
You Didn't Do Your Part
OR—I'm Not Good Enough
Or—Bad Luck Gets The Blame

AT NO TIME DO I SEE THAT
I AM POWERFUL

Therefore,
Even When I Succeed
I Don't Enjoy The Outcome

I Understand Concepts
At The Thinking Level
However, I Don't Get Commitment,
Responsibility, Contribution,
and Living As My Word
At An Internal Gut Level

THE BELIEF HERE IS THAT
IN ORDER FOR ME TO WIN
SOMEONE ELSE HAS TO LOSE!

WIN — LOSE

I Am The Creator of The Game

I CREATE IT ALL

I Create My Interpretation

I Create Beliefs That Empower Me And Others

I Create My Experience Of It All

I Live In The Context Of What If

I Choose and Declare What I Am Committed To

Even If I Fall Down Ten Times, I GET BACK UP,

Get The Support I Need, Take Action Until I Create What I Say I Am Committed To and Win

I Live As My Word

I Focus Out

My Life Is An Invitation To Others

I Am The Creator of The Game

I understand that everyone shifts back and forth among the three different roles.

I don't reach creator and just coast.

The point is to pay attention and be honest about where I am.
If I see I've slipped to participant or observer and want something to be different, I catch myself and shift back to creator.

I Live In The Context Of Contribution

If Something Isn't Working
In A Relationship,
At School,
With Work, Etc.

I Can Do Something To Change

EVERYBODY WINS!

WIN — WIN

Chapter 7

I Create, Therefore I Am

CREATING YOUR LIFE ON PURPOSE

How Commitment, Intention, and Action Intersect To Create Your Results

Intention Is A Powerful Practical Tool Humans Have Been Using For Centuries. The way of being we call intention happens when we give our focus and attention to something we desire and/or need.

> Intention Isn't
> New Age
> Magic Fairy dust!

> The fact that I give it focus actually creates new opportunities.

> By setting an intention
> I am saying that I now am going to focus on this particular desire.

> Setting Intention
> Causes Us To
> Notice Opportunities
> We Wouldn't See
> If We Were
> Traveling and Thinking
> What We Have Always
> Believed and Thought.

THE STREET CORNER OF INTENTION AND GOOD LUCK

There is a misconception out there about "Good Luck" –
Good Luck always happens when intention (opportunity) intersects with action.

Good Luck isn't a sometimes maybe thing
Good Luck is always present
Action has the good luck show up
Because - No matter our intention action creates results.

Life is not a coincidence
Life flows naturally
Look back at your life and just notice
how each step of the journey
has led you to right now.

INTENTION ALWAYS EQUAL RESULTS

The statement that my intentions always equal my results, and that regardless of my intention, actions produce my results, are not contradictory. Our true intentions drive our actions, thereby creating our results. The question to investigate is this:

Are my intentions producing the exact results I want?
There Is A Natural Logical Order
In How Intention and Results Work
Your True Intention will ALWAYS Equal Your Results

BUT

1. ***Your belief systems drive your internal intentions***
2. ***Your thoughts drive your external intentions***

Therefore, it is your job to see that your belief systems are in alignment with your conscious intentions. Otherwise, you are just waiting for magic and with magic you don't have to be responsible. With magic you may or may not get the exact results you were expecting. One day you pull a rabbit out of your hat and the next day the rabbit has disappeared down the rabbit hole.

It's important to wake up to how you create your results through intention. How we create intention has a direct bearing on how your life turns out. First, we develop interpretations and beliefs. Our ego then takes on the task of proving that we are right about the beliefs we have developed around these interpretations.

You wake up one morning and decide you want to be playful today. You want to spend some free happy time with your family today. You are taking the day off to play golf and have a "Free Will" kind of day.

That is your conscious intention.

But wait just a minute! Out of how you view the world (your life interpretations) you have formed a belief that to show love I am a good provider; it's my job to get food on the table. It's not okay to have fun now, but If I work hard and do the right thing, then someday it will be my turn. You have a judgment/interpretation of what makes a good guy versus a lazy guy, the role of a single parent, your role in your marriage etc. and you have turned that into a belief system that rules your way of life.

That, my friend, is your hidden intention

The question here is which intention is stronger: the conscious intention to play today or your hidden intention to be a good provider and not be lazy? Your results are erratic for a logical reason. Sometimes your public, conscious, out in the open, on top of the table intention is stronger. Sometimes you're below the surface, private, unconscious, hidden, I shouldn't feel or act this way intention is stronger. You are in a double bind of which you aren't aware and the stronger intention at any given moment wins this round.

In the story, P.J. and Will had zero chance at the results they consciously stated that they wanted in their marriage as long as their belief system was that, "The Romance Goes Out Of The Marriage In Two Years." In fact, they could not transform from P.J. and Will into Pure Joy and Free Will until they risked discussing and changing the unworkable belief they had about marriage and partnership.

Every One Of Us Absolutely and Always Keeps Our Commitments!

Does that mean they were bad people and uncommitted? Absolutely not! They were keeping their commitments. The problem is that oft times our true commitments are hidden and unconscious. This isn't bad news, because there is a way to know where our true commitments lie. You know that your true commitment will always equal your results. Therefore, if you want to know what you are truly committed to all you ever need do is look at the results you are producing right now. If you aren't producing exactly what you consciously want—quit pretending that you don't know what the unconscious belief system driving you is. I'm not talking sub conscious buried somewhere in deep recesses of your psyche here. There is an unconscious intention that you know you have. You have had it for so long that it is just automatic and running in the background. You know you're breathing but you don't think about it all day long. Breathing is happening in the background automatically as you are giving your attention consciously to something else. Move the unconscious belief to the conscious mind and get it off of cruise control. At that point you have the power to reset the intention to be in alignment with what's important, and sha-zamm you've changed the result.

WHAT ARE YOU PRETENDING NOT TO KNOW!

The intention process as defined here
is based on the premise
that interpretation, thought, and judgment
creates belief:

Conscious Commitments + Unconscious Commitment
= Intention
Conscious Intentions + Unconscious Intentions
= Results
Public Intentions + Hidden Intentions
= Results

ALWAYS - ALWAYS -ALWAYS!

Chapter 8

I Am Aware, Therefore I Am

NIGHT DRIVING

Life is about day and night. I don't care how awesome your life is, sometimes it's sunlight and roses and sometimes it's not. My niece died recently and it was dark inside. It felt awful but that didn't mean I was broken or needed to fix anything—it was what it was. After a bit of space, however, I didn't want the night to last any longer. This passage is about when those night times come.

It's night. You know you want to drive toward possibility. You also know from experience that if you just take off in the midst of the darkness you're bound to hit a tree or worse yet, fall off of the cliff.

YOU NEED LIGHTS
LIGHTS ARE A TOOL OF LIFE TO HELP GUIDE YOU

A SMALL GOOD STEADY FLASHLIGHT WILL HELP YOU LOOK AT YOUR MAP

BUT TO REALLY MASTER DRIVING THE VEHICLE OUT OF THE DARKNESS YOU NEED A POWERFUL SET OF HEADLIGHTS ON THE CAR.

The high beam gives you a long range view.
The low beam helps you focus on things that might block your path right now.

HAVING GOOD HEADLIGHTS GIVES US SUCH THINGS AS:

1. Courage to drive.
2. Hope that we can travel the distance.
3. Faith that we will be ok even though it's night.

Think of the headlights as your belief systems. The headlight has to be in alignment and focus so the light hits the road we're traveling. Awareness is being conscious of our value and beliefs so that we pick the real path we want to travel. Being consciously aware that our headlights are working properly and focused, we know that we know—"THE LIGHT" within us is bright enough to light whatever path we choose to travel.

Are there obstacles? MOST CERTAINLY!!! Get real—Life is our path here. Of course some debris will be in our path. BUT with a good light, traveling the path is an adventure. I wonder what lies around the curve up ahead but I have no worry because my light (beliefs about responsibility and commitment) will warn me of danger in plenty of time. I can navigate over, under, around, or through to reach the destination I'm aiming for.

Our value and belief systems are supposed to help us be, do, and have what we really want. They are not supposed to stop us from our chosen path. Our headlights (conscious awareness) are there to help us stay in alignment with what we want and get us there safely.

If you want your car to serve you well
and last for years to come,
you must change the oil once in awhile,
get a tune up at frequent intervals,
and replace those old tires.

We know about preventive maintenance for our car, we go to the dentist to get our teeth cleaned, and we get a flu shot every year. Why is it that no one teaches us that personal growth tune ups are just as important?

For Information concerning our
life strategies coaching,
parenting classes,
and other seminars near you
Visit us on the web at toniraye.com

PART III

A 30-DAY WORKBOOK AND ACTION PLAN PRESENTED AND CO-AUTHORED BY MICKEY MCQUAID TO GET YOU MOVING FORWARD SO YOUR DESIRED RESULTS SHOW UP NOW!

Many times I've read a book and thought, "Wow, these are great ideas, I'll do something with that." Three months—a year—two years fly by, my life hadn't changed and my thinking was, "I guess all the mumbo jumbo psycho babble stuff is nice in theory but doesn't work in my real life." My outward conversation was very positive but in a tiny small part of my internal conversation my ego sounded like this:

"Yeah, but "those people" (who those people were I don't know), but for sure "those people" don't know my circumstances—my situation—or they'd realize it's harder for me to have positive change happen in my life!" Sure, it's easy for the important teachers that already make buckets of money to talk about the Power of Attraction and stuff like that. But if they had my life I wonder if they'd be able to have things be different.

I can tell you this; for me it was because I often went 99% of the journey toward success (thinking it all through in my head) but that last 1% that required just small follow through and action didn't seem necessary…so I didn't bother with that part.

You've tried lots of things—what if just this once you give yourself permission to take some small spaces of time for yourself everyday for the next 30 days and follow through with the last 1% of what you have started by reading this book?

YOU HAVE CHOICES TO MAKE RIGHT NOW—
THINK THIS THROUGH

Here Are The Options:

1. If you don't follow through with some kinds of small changes, you know from experience that nothing will change. That's not so bad, you'll be okay. How do I know you'll be okay? Because you are already okay just the way you are. If you are 100% satisfied with the results in your life then just reading this book to this point will bring a smile to your face but won't really change anything in the future.

2. You decide to create a routine for yourself where no matter what else is going on you spend a few minutes every day for the next 30 days and you follow through and it doesn't do any good and nothing changes. Well then, you didn't waste much time and you can be proud of the fact that you are a follow-through person.

3. You decide to create a routine for yourself where no matter what else is going on you spend a few minutes every day for the next 30 days and you follow through and only a small something changes. Well then, surely setting a boundary to spend this time on you is worth the time spent even if only for a small change to occur.

4. BUT WHAT IF you follow through (with these small changes every day that build to a whole change) and that transforms your life forever. What a small price to pay for a life worth living. What a small investment in yourself for the adventure and joy of life to renew and grow for you!!

YES YOU CAN!!! ESCAPE FROM WAS!!!

→ 1/3 of your workbook is about looking at and handling your past

→ 1/3 is about correcting and adjusting course in your present

→ 1/3 deals with and begins to propel you toward your future and what you say you are committed to.

Life is like a big jigsaw puzzle—If you leave out 1/3 of the pieces you won't be seeing the whole picture of what's possible for you.

—toniraye

As you move through the next 30 days you are practicing and doing new things. Therefore, be consciously aware of the following:

Your body: Sensations, stress levels (headache or other ache), fatigue, temperature, atmosphere, or renewed energy and vitality. What is my physical self today?

Thoughts: Images, internal conversations, images from my past etc.

Am I having the same internal conversation 30 times in the space of one minute?
Do my thoughts seem new, fresh, and original for me?

Emotions: Relate to my feelings—am I irritable, feeling joy, overwhelm, anger, peace, what?
Don't see this as either good or bad. Say to yourself this is just what is in this moment. I have feelings but they don't own me so all of my feelings are ok. What are my emotions saying about me today?

Hint—when you notice feelings from the emotional plane, ask yourself, "What were my thoughts one second before I noticed that feeling?"

Attitude: What is my state of mind—point of view—am I cynical, optimistic, arrogant, or supportive?
What does my attitude tell me about me today?

Posturing: My outward appearances, facial expression, behavior patterns—I already know this versus I can't learn this and change are two different internal beliefs that produce very different outward postures.

(1) A sneer of disdain and arrogance
(2) A big smile
(3) Downcast eyes, poor posture, etc.
What is my posturing self saying today?

There are certain ways of "being" and actions that will support your results as you do the workbook assignments during the next 30 days:

1. Focus on the end result we are heading toward, instead of how you are getting the job done.

2. Create new personal rules and boundaries for yourself concerning action and follow through.

3. Give yourself permission to dream full out for the next 30 days.

4. Settle for more.

5. Suspend all disbelief about what will work or not.

6. Rely on unforeseen forces and circumstances to support you in all you are doing.

7. Trust in the power of pursuit and BE In Action.

8. Be uncomfortable—recognize that fear can be a good thing – it means you are up to something powerful.

9. Be the gift that you are.

10. Reach out and receive the gifts that others have for you.

11. Make your move before you're ready.

12. You have the answers within you.

    "I SURRENDER TO ME AND THE WISDOM I HAVE."

13. Listen and learn with new ears.

> *"The real voyage of discovery consists not in seeking new landscapes, but in having new eyes."*
> *—Marcel Proust*

DAY 1 – 3

This first assignment is about reflection and getting started properly. On the surface, the story you just read is a simple parable. Now it is time to reflect and see how the story reflects back to your life and your history. Therefore, it may take more than one day to complete this assignment.

1. Priming the Pump: If you haven't answered the questions at the end of each section, I recommend you take a few days to do so.

2. If you have answered the questions, review everything you wrote. Make any changes you want. Has your thinking and/or feelings changed? If so, write about that in your journal.

3. A suggestion: have a good friend read the book, and do the workbook at the same time. That way you can support and encourage each other.

4. Go TODAY and buy a writing journal. This part of your journey is sacred—I suggest you buy something with a cover that speaks to you. Years from now when you pick up your journal and read what you wrote you will be amazed at how much you have grown and changed. Your journal is an important part of this process!

   If you procrastinate for more than 3 days in taking time out of your already busy schedule to start making changes, then the chances are slim that you will get started.

5. NOW! Acknowledge yourself for taking action and getting started.

> *"The minute you settle for less than you deserve, you get even less than you settled for."*
> *—Maureen Dowd*

DAY 4

1. Step I: Think of a person you really admire. This person can be living or deceased. This person can be real or from a movie, cartoon, fictional, or simply from your imagination.

   Step II: Write down 3 things you admire about this person.

   Step III: Write an I AM statement using the 3 qualities you admire in the person you wrote about above.

   Example: I really admire Mickey Mouse.
   1. Because he is over 60 but lives life with joy and adventure.
   2. Because he has imagination.
   3. Because he has lots of energy.

   I am an adventurous, imaginative, energetic woman who is full of joy.

   Example: I really admire Martin Luther King, Jr.
   1. He lived his life with full commitment.
   2. He was totally passionate about what he believed in.
   3. He was powerful in how he communicated so that others believed as well.

   I am a committed, passionate, powerful man
   who is a contribution to the world.

2. The fact is you can't recognize the greatness in someone else unless you have the seeds of that greatness within you. For today live your life full out as if you were at 100% in "being" the I AM statement you wrote.

3. Recognize that however you lived your I AM statement today, It was your 100% for today.

4. Now acknowledge yourself for living and being your I AM statement at your 100% today.

5. Whatever you are feeling and thinking at this minute—write in your journal. Write until everything in your mind is emptied. You will know you've written enough when you feel complete inside. (It could be a sentence—it could be pages.)

6. Sleep with peace tonight.

Before you start your assignment for today, read through and consider the following ideas about criticism and blame:

Idea I: The fact is that you wouldn't recognize things to criticize in others unless you had those same supposed seeds of fault within yourself. You hate seeing those so called "faults" in you. It is easier to look at and blame or criticize others rather than acknowledge that you want to change.

Idea II: As I blame myself for making mistakes I can use the blaming as a way to let myself off the hook. After all, I am exhausted from blaming myself, so now I'm too tired to change anything. "I am so useless that I don't matter. I am so guilty that now I can't take action because if I'm guilty I'm not worthy so there is no need to attempt to change."

When I am blaming myself or others I am displacing energy that could be harnessed to have my life be what I say I am committed to.

> *"You never find yourself until you face the truth."*
> *—Pearl Bailey*

DAY 5

1. Today as you go through your normal routine just notice how often you criticize yourself and/or others.

2. Write a letter to your inner child telling him or her all the things you wanted to hear as a child from your parents. As you write, remember to be loving and supportive, so your child feels treasured and respected. Your inner child is as innocent as a new born babe. There is no criticism noticed or needed here.

3. With your non-dominant hand, allow your inner child to reply to this letter.

4. Start a daily 5-acknowledgement practice today.

   Right before going to bed, for that particular day write a list of 5 things you acknowledge yourself for. Don't stop until you have 5. They can be small things, e.g: I helped a coworker, I didn't yell at someone who cut me off in traffic, I worked out, I called my brother whom I'd been avoiding, etc.

   A trick that will help you to remember this daily is to put your notebook/ journal on your pillow when you get up in the morning. When you come to bed tonight your wonderful self will see your journal waiting. You remember "Wow, I get to acknowledge myself for me and to me."

(a) Think of five things you acknowledge yourself for today
(b) Write all five down
(c) Say all five out loud.

You think the acknowledgement.
You see the acknowledgement on paper.
You hear it spoken.

You want to give your brain every opportunity to notice that you recognize yourself as a valuable contributing human being.

From this day forward think it, write it, say it out loud!

Before starting your next day's assignment, read and consider the following ideas:

We are no longer hunting and scavenging for food and shelter to stay alive. We are in the information age and we have more available to us than at any other time in history. Yet, we are so bombarded and loaded up with data streaming into our brain that our minds become chaotic and cluttered.

Our mind simply tunes out most of what is trying to get through. We are not even aware that our brain is tuning out some things and letting other bits of information become part of our awareness.

So what happens?

There are awesome miracles and opportunities surrounding us every day and we do not notice because there is too much clutter in the atmosphere. There is no room in our life for anything new and exciting because what we already have takes up all the space. The brain thinks that what already "is" must be more important than something new and wondrous. Think of your brain as a big warehouse full to the rafters with inventory. You can't get in new results (stuff) until you make room and move out some of the old (stuff and ideas).

We can't get rid of stress.
We can't sleep.
We can't meditate.
We can't forge ahead to new heights because we are cluttered up with what "is" already too much to handle – too much to cope with.

But not to worry! We don't have to get rid of everything and start from scratch. Somehow our brain re-adjusts even when we un-clutter in small ways. As we make even a little breathing space for our brain, it will reset itself to allow us to attract new things we desire. As we clean out the clutter of what "is" and what we already "have," we actually free up our brain to notice miracles that have always been right there in front of us.

Hint: Part of the purpose of this 30-day journal and the work you are doing is to clean out your brain and make room for new ideas.

Yes you can Escape From Was!!
You are ready to:
Clean up relationships
Clean up your junk
Clear out your brain and open up to strong powerful ideas.

> *"You gain strength, courage, and confidence by every experience in which you really stop to look fear in the face. You must do the thing which you think you cannot do."*
>
> *—Eleanor Roosevelt*

DAY 6

1. Today's assignment is to un-clutter in some way.
   Clean out your closet and donate something to charity or
   Put up the tools laying around the garage or
   Clean up the inside of your car or
   Organize your office.

2. You need to do it yourself, and it needs to be manual labor so your brain pays attention that you are cleaning out the old disorganized and making room for the future.

   For the process to work best, do something that fills up at least 2 trash bags (5 would even be better).

3. Once the clean-out process is complete pay very close attention over the next few days. Be conscious of small miracles and opportunities coming into your awareness.

   Look for miracles and write in your journal about everything that could be a miracle no matter how small it appears on the surface.

4. Take a risk in an important relationship today. Afterwards, write about the experience. (Did I feel empowered, overwhelmed, procrastinating, relieved, etc.)

   This is about cleaning up relationships as well as cleaning up stuff that clutters your life.

5. Continue your 5 daily acknowledgements practice.
   Think it.
   Write it.
   Say it out loud.

> *"A great many people think they are thinking when they are rearranging their prejudices."*
> *—William James*

DAY 7

In the Land of Was, I believe that things and people are locked into certain roles. This creates constant judgments and assessments. As we begin to see ourselves and others in these roles, everything gets locked in place. I no longer need to talk to the people in my life. I simply talk to and deal with the belief systems I have already decided about everything and everyone.

1. HONESTLY (not the politically-correct version) answer the following, either in a conversation with a friend or by writing a paragraph for each.

   Men are ______________________________________ .

   Women are ____________________________________ .

   Money is—or People with Money are ______________________ .

   The world is ____________________________________ .

   Therefore, I must be ______________________________ .

   A frequent phrase about my life is "I have to __________________."

2. What's a specific situation where you feel trapped in your life?

3. What stands in your way preventing you the freedom to enjoy your everyday life?

4. Continue your 5 daily acknowledgements practice.
   Think it.
   Write it.
   Say it out loud.

> *"Treat people as if they were what they ought to be, and you will help them become what they are capable of becoming."*
> *—Goethe*

DAY 8

1. Call a friend or family member you've been meaning to connect with, but never get around to it. Have an authentic conversation. Find out something they're excited about in their life and something they are struggling with.

2. Leave a note on a co-workers desk (or for a neighbor, if you're at home)— someone you have trouble with at work—tell them one thing they are appreciated for. Give the note anonymously.

3. Acknowledge someone else publically. Catch someone doing something good and tell them.

4. Continue your 5 daily acknowledgements practice.
   Think it.
   Write it.
   Say it out loud.

> *"Even if you're on the right track,*
> *if you just sit there you'll get run over."*
> *—Will Rogers*

DAY 9

1. List 3 interactions that you were involved in today.
   Example: I mentioned to my husband/kids/wife etc. that the trash in the kitchen was smelly.

   Now answer the following questions for each of the three interactions you are examining:

   What was my purpose for saying this/doing this?

   What did I want to get?

   Was my communication open, honest, and genuine in this situation?

   How did it turn out?

   If it didn't turn out how can I powerfully change the outcome ASAP?

   If it did turn out as I wanted it to how will I remember what I did that worked?

Be sure to notice whether it worked to the benefit of everyone not just you. In the trash example success would not be that your husband took out the trash. Success might be that you communicated what your need was, he took out the trash because you ask directly and he felt great about your communication because there was no insinuation—no cutting comment—no background judgment that he should have noticed and taken out the trash without you asking, etc., and by the smile on his face you could tell he really loved supporting you by taking out the trash.

2. Write a dialogue between the part of you who is willing to change, and the part of you who is not willing to change.

3. Then list 3 things you are determined to do to make positive changes in your life within one week.

4. Continue your 5 daily acknowledgements practice.
   Think it.
   Write it.
   Say it out loud.

> *"You don't get to choose how you're going to die. Or when. You can decide how you're going to live now."*
> *—Joan Baez*

DAY 10

1. Do at least one of the things you listed yesterday to make a positive change. Share with a friend or write about your experience afterwards.

2. Do something you consider a treat—indulge yourself in some way.

3. Continue your 5 daily acknowledgements practice.
   Think it.
   Write it.
   Say it out loud.

> ***"All the world's a stage, and all the men and women merely players. They have their exits and entrances. And one man in his time plays many parts."***
> ***—William Shakespeare***

DAY 11

I have feelings, but I am not my feelings. Otherwise, if I wake up feeling great, I have a great day. But if I wake up feeling lousy or doubting myself or angry (etc, etc.), I wait to feel better before I take a risk.

1. Write 2 specific examples when you acted by how you felt, and later regretted it.

2. Write 2 specific examples when you risked and lived a commitment even when you didn't feel like it. How did you feel afterwards?

3. Remember the last time you created drama in your life, producing a conflict with another person. In a nutshell, what was the situation?

4. Now answer these questions:
   What was my part in the disruption of the relationship?
   What thoughts/feelings were controlling my actions?
   What could I have done to produce a different result?

5. Continue your 5 daily acknowledgements practice.
   Think it.
   Write it.
   Say it out loud.

Before turning the page to complete today's assignment read and consider the following idea:

INTERPRETATION

"What he/she did was HORRIBLE." No, they just did what they did—you interpret it and then experience it as horrible. Events are just events—there is no such thing as a good or bad event. What you do with it (based on your beliefs) is what YOU do with it. Otherwise we would have the same experience to the same events—and we don't. We make it all up!

The actual facts are what happened. The facts cannot be changed they just are. What I do with the facts and how I combine the facts of what happened today with past facts has the power to create my life as joyous or not.

How you interpret an event will dictate your reactions, feelings, perspective, and the actions you take from there.

Example: Two women—both their husbands leave them for younger women. The first woman is a total victim—my life is ruined, gets pity and agreement from everyone about what a jerk he is, and badmouths him forever. The second woman, after the initial hurt and shock, decides Great! I'm rid of him. And she goes and gets a younger man!

Example: I was driving on the highway and a little old lady cut me off in traffic. My first thought: "What are they thinking to give her a driver's license? We could have all been killed. I'm pissed off."

This reveals a limiting belief that the system is not to be trusted, being a victim of other drivers' actions, and little old ladies that drive are…!

Now the same situation with a different interpretation: A little old lady cuts me off in traffic. "Wow—I'm such a good driver to avoid an accident for me and everyone. I hope she makes it home safely. I probably saved the life of everyone on this highway."

"The truth" is that there were 2 cars on the highway. Everything past the 2 cars is "my story" about the truth.

> *"We who lived in concentration camps can remember the men who walked through the huts comforting others, giving away their last piece of bread. They may have been few in number, but they offer sufficient proof that everything can be taken from a man but one thing: the last of human freedoms—to choose one's attitude in any given set of circumstances—to choose one's own way."*
>
> —*Viktor Frankl*

DAY 12

1. Today's assignment will take 7 days to complete. Every day for the next seven days pick 3 to5 events.
   (a) Notice your initial interpretation.
   (b) Then you are to consciously interpret the event in a completely different way.

2. Continue your 5 daily acknowledgements practice.
   Think it.
   Write it.
   Say it out loud.

> *"Whatever you can do or dream you can, begin it.*
> *Boldness has genius, power, and magic in it."*
> *—Goethe*

DAY 13

Being Aware Of Miracles

1. Write about the opportunities to celebrate that you bypassed yesterday because you did not recognize them as a miracle and joy of life.

2. What are you going to do today and tomorrow to avoid making the same mistakes?

3. Take a 10 minute nature walk with a focus of simply being present—to the sights, sounds, smells, sensations.

4. Set up whatever you need to (an appointment, etc.) to accomplish your second positive change for this week. If possible, accomplish this today.

5. Remember to continue to re-interpret 3 to 5 events.

6. Continue your 5 daily acknowledgements practice.
   Think it.
   Write it.
   Say it out loud.

> *"There is one who kisses, and one who offers a cheek."*
> *—French Proverb*

DAY 14

Giving and Receiving Love

1. Write about what you really want in a relationship.
   (This can be a relationship you already have, or one you don't have yet.) Don't judge what you are supposed to want or not want...just be honest with yourself.

2. Either have a conversation with a friend answering these questions, or write and FILL A PAGE.
   (a) What won't I give?
   (b) What have I stopped risking?

3. Write in detail about something you need to handle, but haven't. (e.g. losing weight for your health). This should be about your relationship with yourself.

   Now answer these questions:
   (a) What are the prices and rewards (there are ALWAYS rewards) for not handling it?
   (b) What are the prices and rewards if I do handle it?
   (c) What do I notice?

4. Remember to continue the assignment to re-interpret 3-5 events from today.

5. Continue your 5 daily acknowledgements practice.
   Think it.
   Write it.
   Say it out loud.

> *"You never lose by loving.*
> *You always lose by holding back."*
> *—Barbara De Angelis*

DAY 15

1. Take a risk in an important relationship today.

2. Now write about the risk you took.

3. Invite 3 to 8 friends to get together within one week to play "Show and Tell."
   (a) Each person brings something that represents a special time or event in their life (a photo, a memento, singing a song, etc).
   (b) When you get together, each person shows it and tells their story.

4. Set up whatever you need to accomplish your third positive change in the next 2 days.

5. Remember to continue the assignment to re-interpret 3 to 5 events from today.

6. Continue your 5 daily acknowledgements practice
   Think it.
   Write it.
   Say it out loud.

"To forgive is to set a prisoner free and discover the prisoner was you."
—unknown

"Forgiveness means that you do not carry the baggage of an experience. When you choose not to forgive, the experience that you do not forgive sticks with you…forgiveness means that you do not hold others responsible for your experiences… When you forgive you release critical judgment of yourself as well as others."
Gary Zukav, author of "The Seat of the Soul"

DAY 16

Forgiveness is so important that I have used two quotes.

1. Forgiveness is one of the most important lessons we can learn in life. Write about what forgiveness means to you. Don't simply write about the good part of forgiveness. Write about every part of what you think concerning forgiveness.

   Example: If I forgive it opens the door for the same thing to happen. Trust and forgiveness might be all mixed together somehow.

2. Search your soul and be internally honest here! When you decide not to forgive what feelings and/or actions do you take?

2. You are likely to be more purely honest here if you just laugh at yourself for right now. Try exaggerating your statement as to what you do and/or feel. Accept and love this part of you...not for the purpose of letting yourself off the hook but sometimes in life just laughing at our behavior helps us change it and eradicate it forever. When we criticize and judge our behavior we are much more likely to bury it—not even recognize that it exists—and then we continue to practice and repeat behavior unconsciously that doesn't even get us the results we say we want.

   Examples:
   (a) I am so powerful at protecting myself from hurt that I withdraw my love, approval, communication etc.
   (b) What I really really love about myself is that I can go to protection and/or get defensive about other things. I am so macho—I just fight back.
   (c) I love to practice passive aggression and go to subtle revenge.
   (d) I love to practice passive aggression and go to all out revenge.
   (e) I am so controlling that I don't have to worry about forgiveness 'cause I never get hurt.

3. List 3 people/situations you have forgiven, and what it opened up for you and them.

4. Make a list of the people you choose not to forgive, and for what you don't forgive them (be sure to include yourself).
   Write about what not forgiving is costing you in each of these relationships.
   What rewards do you receive by not forgiving?

Example: The sympathy I receive from others as a result of my continued victimhood

I get to cause the other person to feel guilty because if I am miserable and they caused it—they must really be the scum of the earth.

Martyr's are heroes right? If I'm the martyr I must be a good person.

I get to be right in my belief that they are wrong!!!!

5. The great news about forgiveness is that it only takes one person—YOU. Out of the work you've just done, are you now going to forgive someone you had been unwilling to forgive before? Who have you decided to forgive?

6. Remember to continue the assignment to re-interpret 3 to 5 events from today.

7. Continue your 5 daily acknowledgements practice.
   Think it.
   Write it.
   Say it out loud.

Before turning the page to complete today's assignment read and consider the following idea:

GENEROUS LISTENING

Do you think you're a good listener?

Let's explore why we may not be listening

1. Most of us don't listen completely because we think it means we agree with what's being said.

2. Instead of hearing what someone says, whether we agree or not, we are busy rehearsing what our reply will be. Therefore, even if we don't interrupt, we aren't actually listening. Before someone finishes speaking, we are usually already thinking of our response or our judgment/opinion of what they're saying. Do you notice you interrupt people or space out?

3. In addition to how I listen it is useful to pay attention to how, why, when, and how much I speak. Do you make sure people hear you accurately? How many times have you said—about a coworker or family member—I TOLD them...then you're angry or a victim about what they didn't do—when you never checked to see if they heard you accurately to begin with.

4. As the result of an early childhood experience, I felt I wasn't heard. At times in my adult life, I tend to talk too much without realizing it. I just want to make sure I am heard and I always have a lot to say.

Idea: If someone you care about has this problem, try just asking, "Do you feel like I am hearing what you are saying?" Or, simply start a reply with, "I'm hearing what you are saying."

5. Sometimes we have a problem listening because we are so determined that we are right there is no space or need to hear what someone else has to say. After all, if I am right and you are wrong and I already know I am right…then what a waste of my time to still be listening.

Here is what is great—listening is a skill, and if you're committed to improve, you can practice and you can improve.

> *"To listen well is as powerful a means of influence as to talk well, and is as essential to all true conversation."*
> *—Chinese Proverb*

DAY 17

1. Create an agreement with a friend to take about 30 minutes to practice the following assignment with you (preferably in person). Context of Genuine Listening: being 100% responsible to hear someone accurately and be 100% responsible to be heard accurately.

   Step I: Label 2 pieces of paper. One is marked receiving. One is marked sending.

   Step II: One of you will start talking about something you're excited about or struggling with. You will hold the sending card. This anchors in that it is your turn to send.

   Step III: Whoever starts by listening holds the receiving card in their hand. This will help you anchor in the fact that your job now is only to generously listen and receive communication. Give full attention (If you get distracted, stop them and ask them to repeat).

   Step IV: After about a minute (it's NOT a memory test) jump in and repeat back EXACTLY what you heard them say. Have them correct you if you don't get it right.

   Step V: Have them continue talking and repeat I and II.

Step VI: After 5 minutes, reverse roles. Then share together what you noticed. It's normal if it is awkward at first. Repeat 2 more times.

HINT: This is a really valuable exercise to practice with your children or with your parents. Yes the purpose of the exercise is to help you practice generous listening. But an added benefit is that in any relationship people love it when you take the time to actually hear them.

2. Remember to continue the assignment to re-interpret 3 to 5 events from today.

3. Continue your 5 daily acknowledgements practice.
   Think it.
   Write it.
   Say it out loud.

> ***"I have made a ceaseless effort not to ridicule, not to bewail, not to scorn human actions, but to understand."***
> ***—Baruch Spinoza***

DAY 18

Empathy

1. The following assignment will continue for the next 7 days.

   Every day pick a frustrating relationship interaction. It could be the waitress that forgets to bring you coffee. For the first few days pick small situations that happened that day. Days 5, 6, and 7 pick major interactions of more lasting importance. The bigger events can be from your past or present.

   Step I: Put yourself in the other person's shoes, and come up with several feelings the other person has. DO NOT move to step 3 until you can honestly feel empathy for the other person (empathy is not agreement). If at first you can't feel empathy, pick an easier situation.

   Step II: Be sure to repeat out loud the feelings that the other person must be experiencing. We often just talk to ourselves inside our head. When you say it out loud you might see their feelings as more real. Go to the extreme as you put yourself in the other persons shoes!!

Example:
Wow, Sally must be feeling overwhelmed with the sudden breakfast rush.
I wonder if I were in her shoes if I would feel unappreciated by customers who are so busy they forget to even take one small second to smile?
Sally must get irritated at people who are slightly impolite and rude during her day.
Sally must feel yucky from constantly carrying people's left over garbage and plates. I bet her job isn't very rewarding for her emotionally or financially.

Step III: Now look in the mirror and repeat these words out loud!! (No matter how silly you perhaps feel):

"Wow, it sure looks like _________ has a problem.
That is so sad for him/her.
He/she must be feeling _______ and _________.
But ONE THING I KNOW FOR SURE is that even though _________ might have a problem,
_________'s problems do not cause my problems or reactions.
Because I create my experience and life problems out of my own beliefs and my way of being."

FOR EXAMPLE: My boss, "Mr. Hard-as-Nails," came into my office today and was so demanding and critical. "Wow, it sure looks like Mr. Hard-as-Nails has a problem. That is so sad for him.

a) It must be so hard for him to carry the burden that he is afraid to trust others to get things right.
b) That must be so exhausting for him.
c) It must be sad that he can't relax and enjoy al the precious moments

of life that happen throughout the day.

But ONE THING I KNOW FOR SURE is that even though ________ might have a problem, his problems do not cause my problems or reactions because I create my experience out of my own beliefs and my way of being."

2. Everyday for this week, after you complete the exercise write in your journal (or share with a friend) about how you felt when the situation occurred, and how you felt after you evoked empathy and took responsibility.

3. Remember to continue the assignment to re-interpret 3 to 5 events from today.

4. Continue your 5 daily acknowledgements practice.
   Think it.
   Write it.
   Say it out loud.

> *"Life consists in what a man is thinking of all day."*
> *—Ralph Waldo Emerson*

DAY 19

Over the past week you have worked on major mental aspects of life that keep us stuck in the "Land of Was." You have been thinking, writing, and working on your behavior around forgiveness and empathy. In addition, for the past 7 days you have been learning to re-interpret daily events. You are ready to move to the next level in "being" Pure Joy.

1. Look back through your journal and consider all you wrote about forgiveness and empathy. If you notice new thoughts write them down now.

2. In light of the work you have done in the area of forgiveness, empathy and/or interpretation can you think of any events from your past where it would be valuable and empowering to re-interpret the event?

   Again as human beings we are interpretation machines and if we are going to make everything up why not take this moment to make up something that will empower you instead of having this past "Living in the Land of Was" event continue to negatively affect your present and future.

   Example: In childhood I experienced sexual child abuse. I don't need to excuse it in order to move on with my life. I do need to release it and re-interpret the meaning of the event.

Interpretation #1: Something really terrible and devastating happened to me. Life isn't safe and I'd better be careful. People don't have my best interest at heart so I'd better be darn sure that I take care of myself.... because no one else is likely to help me.

Interpretation #2: What that person did was wrong. It is sad that I didn't know how to tell someone so I would feel safe at that time. I don't have to be happy about bad things that happened in the past. But from what happened to me, I see a need in the world where I can make a difference. I can teach and support others in learning how to get help, and communication has the ability to prevent things like this for other children. I am a teacher and I can be sure that it isn't swept under the carpet and not talked about. In fact, I see that the contribution for my entire life—my entire life's work springs up because this event happened. I matter, I make a difference because of some of my past life experiences.

RE-INTERPRET SOMETHING SMALL OR LARGE RIGHT NOW THAT OCCURRED IN YOUR PAST!!

Now repeat the following: I don't have the power to change the past but Albert Einstein said, "There are only two ways to live your life. One is as though nothing is a miracle. The other is as though everything is a miracle." DECLARE NOW—How I choose to live my life is________.

3. Continue to practice your daily empathy assignment.

4. Continue your 5 daily acknowledgements practice.
   Think it.
   Write it.
   Say it out loud.

You are now moving to the Land of Becoming.

The next days of your journal and action work will prepare you for your future.

> ***"Only those willing to go too far***
> ***will know how far they can really go."***
> ***—Chuck Yaeger***

DAY 20

1. List 3 dreams you had for your life when you were a child.

2. Giving yourself complete permission, list 3 dreams you have for your life now. Go into specific detail and fill a page.

3. Continue to practice your daily empathy assignment.

4. Continue your 5 daily acknowledgements practice.
   Think it.
   Write it.
   Say it out loud.

> ***"We must not, in trying to think about how we can make a difference, ignore the small daily difference we can make which, over time, add up to big differences that we often cannot foresee."***
>
> ***—Marian Wright Edelman***

DAY 21

1. Write (by hand) a letter to someone who has made a difference in your life to acknowledge them. Mail it. (Hey you—yeah you, really mail it. Don't text it, how about you write a real note on real paper and mail it? Sending a message that you actually took time to write—what a concept!)

2. List 3 things you are determined to do to make a positive change in your life within 6 days.

3. Do the first one.

4. Do 3 random acts of kindness today. (One gets to be anonymous) Example: Let someone go ahead of you in the supermarket check-out line.

5. Continue to practice your daily empathy assignment.

6. Continue your 5 daily acknowledgements practice.
   Think it.
   Write it.
   Say it out loud.

> ***"It isn't where you came from;***
> ***it's where you're going that counts."***
> ***—Ella Fitzgerald***

DAY 22

1. What exactly is Your Purpose in Life? Write 2 pages with specific examples.

2. What kind of person would you need to be, for real, to create it?

   Example: passionate, honest, loving, courageous, understanding, etc....

3. Continue to practice your daily empathy assignment.

4. Continue your 5 daily acknowledgements practice.
   Think it.
   Write it.
   Say it out loud.

> *"Not knowing when the dawn will come,*
> *I open every door."*
> *—Emily Dickinson*

DAY 23

1. Set up your second positive change to accomplish tomorrow.

2. Now go do something fun—REALLY FUN—that you used to love doing as a child.

3. Take off the rest of the day from any other assignments.

> *"The best way to predict the future is to create it."*
> *—Peter Drucker*

DAY 24

1. Close your eyes and visualize what you want your life to be like one year from today.

   Step 1: Write it all down. You can't think this one out or talk it out. Talk with someone if you want but also be sure to write and describe in detail your vision for your life. Include your experience of yourself and life, relationships, career/school, spiritual, health, finance, etc.

   Step 2: After one hour or more, reread your one year vision.
   Make any adjustments you choose.

   Step 3: Now go to the future.
   It is one year from now.
   You have created EVERYTHING you wrote.

   Now look back and see all the steps you took to create about it. Write in detail. (It is easier to be at the top of the mountain and look down and see the path you took to get there, than be at the bottom looking up—wondering how you're ever going to make it)

2. Accomplish your second positive change.

3. Take an action step to improve your financial situation.

For example: cancel a credit card, write a budget you're going to keep, set a tax appointment, etc.

4. Continue to practice your daily empathy assignment.

5. Continue your 5 daily acknowledgements practice.
   Think it.
   Write it.
   Say it out loud.

> *"The soul should always stand ajar.*
> *Ready to welcome the ecstatic experience."*
> *—Emily Dickinson*

DAY 25

1. Go to a quiet place by yourself.
   Think of something from the past or present that is really funny.
   Start to laugh quietly.
   Let it bubble up more.
   Laugh out loud.
   Laugh for at least 1 minute.

   Now notice something about your the physical self (face hair etc.).
   Notice your thoughts about joy and laughing.
   Notice your feelings .

2. Now pick up a piece of fruit or a flower.
   Take at least 3 whole minutes to examine it and explore it.
   The smell.
   The texture.
   The miracle and joy of it all.

3. Continue your 5 daily acknowledgements practice.
   Think it.
   Write it.
   Say it out loud.

> *"One must care about a world one will not see."*
> *—Bertrand Russell*

DAY 26

1. Meditate and think about what are you contributing to your world where you may never fully see the fruits of your labor—yet you continue to contribute anyway?

2. Meditate and think about what legacy are you creating for your children's children to inherit?

3. Now fill 2 pages or have a detailed conversation with a friend.

4. Set up your third positive change to accomplish tomorrow.

5. Continue your 5 daily acknowledgements practice.
   Think it.
   Write it.
   Say it out loud.

> *"Life is either a daring adventure or nothing."*
> *—Helen Keller*

DAY 27

1. Write a 2 month intention statement about what you are committed to creating that will support you in having a life worth living.

   Include goals for all important areas of your life—e.g self, career/school, family, financial, health, spiritual, community, etc.

3. Now map out the action steps and check points to have them accomplished—starting at week 8 and working backwards

   Example: Week 8 = 10 pounds lost
   Week 7 = 9 pounds lost
   Week 6 = 7 pounds lost

4. Continue your 5 daily acknowledgements practice.
   Think it.
   Write it.
   Say it out loud.

> *"If you don't know where you are going,*
> *you'll end up someplace else."*
> *—Yogi Berra*

DAY 28

1. Give a friend a copy of your action plan. Ask them for HONEST feedback (this part is on track, this is vague, get more specific, etc.) Adjust action plan as needed.

2. Begin your action plan.

TAKE ACTION ON YOUR PLAN

TAKE ACTION ON YOUR PLAN

TAKE ACTION ON YOUR PLAN

3. Continue your 5 daily acknowledgements practice.
Think it.
Write it.
Say it out loud.

> ***"The ability to convert ideas to things is the secret to outward success."***
> ***—Henry Ward Beecher***

DAY 29

1. TAKE ACTION ON YOUR PLAN

   TAKE ACTION ON YOUR PLAN

   TAKE ACTION ON YOUR PLAN

2. STRETCH yourself. Accomplish at least twice as much as you were originally planning to today After you have, write what your experience was, and what you learned for yourself.

3. Continue your 5 daily acknowledgements practice.
   Think it.
   Write it.
   Say it out loud.

> *"Never give up, for that is just the place and time that the tide will turn."*
>
> *—Harriet Beecher Stowe*

DAY 30

1. GO BACK TO THE BEGINNING OF YOUR WORKBOOK AND READ THE WAYS OF BEING PAGE.

2. Check in with yourself to see how many of these ways of being are now becoming comfortable habits for you.

5. Write about how your "Way of Being" is changing your life and the life of everyone you touch.

6. TAKE ACTION ON YOUR PLAN

7. Continue your 5 daily acknowledgements practice.
   Think it.
   Write it.
   Say it out loud.

ESCAPE FROM WAS

From: Gregory S. Downing
To: Toniraye
Regarding: A Letter To My Mom About Legacy and Contribution

Dear Mom,

So often as you live day-to-day it becomes easy to forget the people who have had a positive impact on your life. I want you to know that not a day goes by that I don't thank the Universe for you, mom.

You have taught me so much about living life on my terms. You instilled the knowledge that I can be anything I want to be, and achieve all that I want to achieve. Your life lessons have allowed me to become a better father to my children, and given me the confidence to accomplish great things both personally and professionally.

Your passion for living and commitment to family has made us all stronger and brought us closer together. Through a shared vision our family now marches forward creating a legacy focused on helping others Escape From Was, and experience the life of their dreams.

I am so proud to be your son and to know that while our work here is not yet done what we are building each and every day together will help generations to come. Thank you for allowing me to be a part of it all.

Your loving son,

Greg

LaVergne, TN USA
22 October 2009

161722LV00003B/12/P

9 781936 051304